Mother Ann Lee

Mother Ann Lee
Morning Star of the Shakers

Nardi Reeder Campion

University Press of New England
Hanover and London

The University Press of New England

is a consortium of universities in New England dedicated to publishing scholarly and trade works by authors from member campuses and elsewhere. The New England imprint signifies uniform standards for publication excellence maintained without exception by the consortium members. A joint imprint of University Press of New England and a sponsoring member acknowledges the publishing mission of that university and its support for the dissemination of scholarship throughout the world. Cited by the American Council of Learned Societies as a model to be followed, University Press of New England publishes books under its own imprint and the imprints of

Brandeis University
Brown University
Clark University
University of Connecticut
Dartmouth College
Middlebury College
University of New Hampshire
University of Rhode Island
Tufts University
University of Vermont
Wesleyan University

©1976, 1990 by Nardi Reeder Campion. Originally published in 1976 as *Ann the Word.*

Printed in the United States of America

⊗

Library of Congress Cataloging-in-Publication Data

Campion, Nardi Reeder.
    Mother Ann Lee : morning star of the Shakers / Nardi Reeder
Campion.
        p. cm.
    Rev. ed. of: Ann the Word. c1976.
    Includes bibliographical references and index.
    ISBN 0-87451-527-0 (alk. paper)
    1. Lee, Ann, 1736-1784. 2. Shakers—Biography. 3. Women
evangelists—United States—Biography. I. Campion, Nardi Reeder.
Ann the Word. II. Title.
BX9793.L4C355   1990
289'.8'092—dc20
    [B]   90-50305
                                                                          CIP

5 4 3 2

For
Husband,
with Love,
and
with Reason

The inner life is twofold, embracing repentance —
confessing and forsaking all sin — and regeneration —
living according to the teachings and practice of Jesus
Christ.

From the Doctrine of the
American Society of Shakers

Happy are those who dream of dreams and are ready to
pay the price to make them come true.

His Eminence Leon-Joseph Cardinal Suenens

'Tis the Gift To Be Simple

'Tis the gift to be simple, 'tis the gift to be free,
'Tis the gift to come down where you ought to be,
And when we find ourselves in the place just right,
'Twill be in the valley of love and delight.
When true simplicity is gained,
To bow and to bend we shan't be ashamed.
To turn, turn will be our delight
'Till by turning, turning we come round right.

Shaker Dance Song

Contents

Foreword

It seems hard to believe that Ann Lee and Abigail Adams, to my mind eighteenth-century America's most extraordinary women, were close contemporaries. They were only eight years apart in age, with Ann the elder, and they shared the same New England corner of the country, but they seem to have come from different worlds — one so accessible, one of such mystery.

We know what Abigail Adams looked like, what her houses and some of her possessions were like, and, above all, what she thought and felt, thanks to her voluminous correspondence. In contrast, there is very little left to reveal Ann Lee's life. There are no portraits of her. We know of a room or two where she stayed, some scraps of fabric from her dress, a chair in which she is said to have sat. What we know of her thoughts and feelings makes her more remote, not closer. Most of us could enjoy a dinner conversation with Abigail Adams, who was keenly interested in the world and was friends with the likes of Thomas Jefferson and Benjamin Franklin. I don't know what most of us could say to Ann Lee, who turned her back on the world and communicated with angels and spirits.

In their own time, the lives of these two women were a study in contrasts. Abigail Smith Adams was a child of small-town New England privilege and a true daughter of the Enlightenment. Her father, a minister, took pains to educate her. She read widely throughout her life. Her husband was a Harvard graduate and a lawyer. Abigail was a woman of words, and of the rational kind of thought that finds its best expression in words.

Ann Lee Standerin was of the working class, born in an English factory city. Her husband and father were both blacksmiths. Her brothers thought it was all right to beat her when they didn't like what she preached. Ann worked in textile mills and was illiterate. The only writing we have from her hand is the X she put by her name on her marriage license. Although Ann could be persuasive when she spoke, as her converts later testified, her power was expressed most forcefully in other ways — in her gaze, her demeanor, the way her body shook when she was filled with spiritual zeal. She was known to call herself "Ann the Word."

The two women never met, but their lives intersected on American soil for ten years in the late eighteenth century. In May 1774, at age thirty-eight, Ann Lee took the most momentous step of her life. Driven by her conviction that a new order of spiritual life could be established in America, she left England, accompanied by eight followers, including her husband. In June of the same year, John Adams left New England to take part in the Continental Congress. Abigail was as ardent as her husband in supporting the creation of a new political order, but as the young mother of three, it was her place to stay home and keep the farm operating.

It is fascinating to me that, in spite of their differences, Ann and Abigail sought something similar — a change from the established order. For Abigail, the work would come from within the system. She wanted the laws to change, but she accepted the fact that they would still be made and enforced by men — American men, not English men. Today Abigail has gained a kind of positive notoriety for ordering John to "Remember the Ladies" and for exhorting him to treat women more equitably under the new system of laws, but for all her intelligence and spirit, Abigail was a most conventional woman. Her role was that of helpmate in practical and political matters.

How different Ann Lee was. In a world that taught women to be obedient and to "keep within compass" and whose church and state made obedience the only acceptable course of behavior, Ann Lee violated the laws of men and convention. She was a separated woman who took back her maiden name after her husband left her. She was the acknowledged leader and spokeswoman of her small group, which included men. She preached in public and went into churches to interrupt services. She was arrested, imprisoned, and physically and verbally abused for what she preached. Her behavior was not socially acceptable. Her opponents called her a witch or a whore, while her followers believed her to be a saint or the Christ spirit incarnate in a woman, but no one could have called her a "lady."

Today, more than two hundred years later, we are the inheritors of the state that Abigail Adams's husband worked to create. The founding fathers did not "remember the ladies" in their new laws, nor did they abolish slavery. It has taken this nation two centuries to legislate equality across the board, and we still have much to do in the arena of human rights. While it is technically possible for someone who is not male, heterosexual, or white to become president, such an event is hardly more conceivable in this country today than it was when Abigail Adams and Ann Lee lived.

Ann Lee was concerned with souls, not politics. Her single question was, "Do you want to be saved?" If the answer was yes, nothing else mattered — not gender, age, color, or any other factor. Ironically, in divorcing herself from the new American republic, Ann Lee established a world that went radically beyond the new United States in its theories and practice of equality.

In August 1784, Abigail Adams made a momentous trip of her own, crossing the Atlantic to reunite with her husband and more closely share his life and political career while he was in Europe. A month later, Ann Lee was dead of the long-term effects of injuries she had suffered in the Old World and the New.

In the end, we remember Abigail Adams not for who she was herself, but because she was someone's wife and someone's mother. The men in her life were presidents, to be sure, and so her experience was extraordinary in that regard, but her importance after all was as an appendage. Without John Adams or John Quincy Adams, what would we really know of her?

But we remember Ann Lee for herself and for the Shaker world that she helped bring into being. It is a privilege to remember her, this bold, uncomfortable, unconventional woman, and to express gratitude to Nardi Reeder Campion for telling the story of Ann Lee's life.

Pittsfield, Massachusetts   June Sprigg
April 1990

Preface

A Pioneer of the Spirit

Few episodes in all history are as radical or as colorful as the rise of the Shakers. The United Society of Believers in Christ's Second Appearing, as they were called, was a communal, celibate, ecstatic religious sect that flourished in America during the nineteenth century. Astonishingly, it sprang from the charismatic personality of one obscure, illiterate woman, Ann Lee.

Ann's magnificent obsession was Jesus Christ. A born leader, she was convinced the world's problems would be solved if she could persuade people to follow his example literally. More astonishingly, after a mystical vision, her soul "broke through to God" and she believed she was the second coming of Christ, in the body of a woman. To her devout followers she was Ann, the Word of God made manifest — the female Christ. It is important to add that the Shakers did not consider Jesus divine. To them, both Christ and Mother Ann, the female Christ, possessed the divine Christ-spirit, but neither was a god.

What motivated thousands of Americans to abandon their families and renounce all sex and all worldly possessions to become Shakers? Some may have wanted to escape the tension and responsibility of family life. At one time, a "respectable" way to divorce a spouse was to join the Shakers. Others yearned for commitment to a totally demanding faith that would permeate every facet of their lives. Striving for a "closer walk with God," they risked everything to follow Mother Ann's instruction: "You must seek your true religion where your deep bliss is."

Ann Lee lived only forty-eight years, from 1736 to 1784, but eventually she became the spiritual leader of thousands. With incredible boldness, she strove to chart the most difficult of all worlds to enter — the world of the spirit. In the process, she founded one of the most successful experiments in communal living the world has ever seen.

Mother Ann was to have a much wider influence than such popular colonial heroines as Molly Pitcher, Betsy Ross, and Martha Washington. Her dream for humanity exceeded all patriotic boundaries. It is odd that Ann Lee has never been recognized as one of the first — if not *the* first — women in this country to possess power and to use it for the liberation of other women.

Consider these verifiable facts : Born in the eighteenth century, when nearly all women were the possessions of men, a deeply religious Ann Lee spread her faith by daring to be an evangelist. She preached in the streets, since no woman could set foot in a pulpit, and was thrown into jail for it. In the grim mill town of Manchester, England, she led evangelical services of worship that included public confession of sin, speaking in tongues, esctatic dancing — and went to jail for it. After marriage, she defied convention by using her own name instead of her husband's. Most importantly, she founded a religious order, which became The United Society of Believers in Christ's Second Appearing — the Shakers.

To escape British tyranny, Mother Ann took her small band of disciples on a perilous fifty-nine-day voyage across the ocean to an unknown land called America. In the wilderness of upstate New York, she and her followers carved out the first Shaker settlement. During the American Revolution, Mother Ann, a dedicated pacifist, stood unequivocally for nonresistance, quoting Jesus: "Love your enemies, bless them that curse you, do good to them that hate you, and pray for them which despitefully use you, and persecute you." Again she was sent to prison.

Later she trekked by carriage and sleigh throughout New England, enduring unbelievable hardship and persecution in order to attract new members to the Society of Believers. This Society, ruled by *both* women and men, was based on a conviction that God had to be *both* male and female. To generations of followers, she became the female Christ. Clearly, Mother Ann Lee was a morning star, not just for the Shakers, but for the independence of women in the New World.

Contemporary records of Mother Ann's life are meager. No one dreamed that this obscure, poverty-stricken, voluble, zealous woman would start an influential religious movement. The most valuable accounts of Mother Ann's story were written after she died. To get the whole story, a biographer must sift through three early books: *The Testimony of Christ's Second Appearing* by Benjamin S. Youngs, published in 1808; *A Summary View of the Millennial Church* by Calvin Green and Seth Y. Wells, 1823; and *Testimonies of the Life, Character, Revelations and Doctrines of Our Ever Blessed Mother Ann Lee, and the Elders with Her,* 1816. These books record in detail the extraordinary life of Mother Ann. Having been compiled by devoted followers, they are hardly impartial, yet they draw a vivid picture of her, based on interviews with her contemporaries.

Unfortunately, no actual likeness of Mother Ann exists. Peter Bishop, of Montague, Massachusetts, testified that she was the most beautiful woman he ever saw. Others spoke of her compelling blue eyes and inner radiance. One disciple lauded her "cool serenity in danger and rare elevation of soul." Clearly, her kind of beauty was not skin-deep.

Even discounting the Shaker's childlike naiveté about the supernatural, we are left with a courageous woman who triumphed over nearly insuperable odds. The record of her life remains riveting. Mother Ann, the visionary, saw what was wrong with society and knew that *all of its ills were connected.* She believed the primary problem was the inhumanity of human beings. (She probably would have disliked Robert Burns's phrase, *"man's* inhumanity to *man."*) She knew the sickness of society could be healed only by a radical change in values — with the support of a new spiritual community. The Millenium would take time — she knew that. But for Mother Ann, the tangled skeins of the present day are as nothing when measured against the endless tapestry of eternity.

This immensely brave visionary woman, Mother Ann Lee, established a Shaker society where, for a time, men and women were able to escape from the chains of competition, materialism, sexism, and self-gratification and live their lives according to Saint Paul's words in the Book of Acts: "All that believed were together, and had all things common . . . and were of one heart, and of one soul."

Hanover, N.H.   N.R.C.
April 1990

Author's Note

On a blustery winter day in the 1970s, our friends Cornelia and Andrew Fisher launched me on my Shaker journey. They took my husband and me to an exciting auction of Shaker artifacts at the Darrow School in New Lebanon, New York. We watched, open-mouthed, as museum and curators bid astronomical amounts of money for an original chair or a tiny oval box crafted by Shakers. I decided I wanted to learn about the "United Society of Believers in Christ's Second Appearing."

In the Darrow School library, I found an ancient book about the founder of the Shakers, Mother Ann Lee. I had never heard of her. But the very idea that an eighteenth-century woman had been known as the female Christ was riveting. The next day I started to study the Shakers.

My book would never have seen the light of day were it not for the gentle needling, sometimes heavy prodding, always enthusiastic interest of my best editor, best friend, best husband, Tom Campion. His unwavering support means everything to me.

I am deeply indepted to Alan T. Gaylord, Henry Winkler Professor of Anglo-Saxon and English Language and Literature at Dartmouth College, who suggested to the University Press of New England the reissuing of this book, and to my dear friend and mentor, Noel Perrin, also of the Dartmouth English department, who kept me going through thin and thick. The fact that these two brilliant scholars were able to slide down from the rarefied atmosphere of Academe to help me was giddy encouragement.

Julia Fifield, a member of the Board of Trustees of Canterbury Shaker Village, with her irrestible enthusiasm, has been instrumental in the book's publication, and I thank her. I want to thank as well Beverly Gaylord, an authority on Shaker music, and Flo Morse, the author of *The Shakers and the World's People.*

Other editors, supporters, and kind critics to whom I am indebted are our daughter Cissa Campion; my brother Red Reeder ("King of the Literary Frontier"); my sister-in-law Dorothea Darrah Reeder ("The Duchess of Accuracy"); our great-niece, Heather McCutcheon; John G. Keller, Vice President of Little, Brown & Company; Winfred E. A. Bernhard of the University of Massachusetts; and Henry Steele Commager, walking reference library.

I am indebted to the Robert Frost Library at Amherst College, the William A. Neilson Library at Smith College and the Baker Library at Dartmouth College, for their remarkable generosity with valuable treasures and talents. Judy Speidel and Patrick Sullivan, of the University of Massachusetts School of Education, shared with me research done for their slide-tape presentation, "The Shaker Legacy."

Special thanks to two gifted helpers, also from Dartmouth: Mary Kate Schroeder, class of 1992, editor par excellence; and Thomas Summerall, class of 1988, "The Wizard of Electronic Oz."

One Shaker authority had an unwitting influence on this book: Amy Bess Miller, who — with foresight and determination comparable to Mother Ann's — saved the Hancock Shaker Community from extinction. It was there that my Shaker enthusiasm caught fire.

The late William L. Lassiter, a well-known collector and an authority on Shaker architecture, shared a memorable afternoon with us in his Albany home crammed with Shaker antiques that are now in the Metropolitan Museum. He spoke of Mother Ann as if he knew her.

I journeyed to the Sabbathday Lake Shaker Community in Maine, for a seminar commemorating the two-hundredth anniversary of Mother Ann's arrival in America. It was beautifully conducted by Theodore E. Johnson, resident scholar and sage. The three days I spent at Sabbathday lake changed not only my book, but my life.

N.R.C.

Mother Ann Lee

Chapter One

Ann Lee of Toad Lane

How little can the rich man know
Of what the poor man feels,
When Want, like some dark demon foe,
Nearer and nearer steals!

He never saw his darlings lie
Shivering, the grass their bed;
He never heard the maddening cry
Daddy, a bit of bread!

— Old Manchester Song

In 1736, on February 29, that mysterious calendar day that surfaces only once in four years, a daughter was born to John Lees and his wife in their dingy lodging on Toad Lane in the oldest quarter of Manchester, England. At her birth there was nothing to indicate her remarkable destiny. Yet this baby girl, Ann Lee of Toad Lane, was one day to have thousands of devout followers who thought of her as the female Christ.

In *Testimonies Concerning the Character and Ministry of Mother Ann Lee,* the book of reminiscences about Ann collected from the people who knew her, Ann's parents are described as poor but honest laborers. Her father, John Lees (the *s* was later dropped) was a blacksmith who had to work as a tailor at night to eke out a meager living for his family. He was "respectable in character, moral in principle, honest and punctual in his dealings, and industrious in business." Her mother was "esteemed as a strictly religious and very pious woman." As often happened in those days, the mother's name was not even recorded.

Of Ann's youth, little is known. She was the second of the Lees' eight children. The registry of Christ Church in Manchester documents Ann Lee's private baptism on June 1, 1742, when she was six years old. It also notes the baptisms of several of her seven brothers and sisters, but aside from this nothing of the early years has come to light.

But of Ann's early surroundings, a great deal is known. Manchester, a black, sprawling city in the center of England, was a place most people preferred to think did not exist. It was a disgrace. The wealth of its textile mills was built on degradation and poverty. The laborers lived close to the mills in unspeakable squalor, while the mill owners lived out in the country, the windows of their elegant Georgian homes facing the rolling green meadows and beautiful woods of Lancashire. The owners allowed themselves to see as little as possible of the workers' misery.

Along with other children in that godforsaken city, Ann Lee went to work in the mills when she was eight years old. There was no question of going to school; the opportunity simply did not exist. Ann did not learn to read or write then, or ever. Like most intelligent illiterates, she developed a strong memory, and in later life her recall of the Bible was prodigious.

Testimonies describes the young Ann as an attractive girl, short and somewhat plump, with light chestnut-brown hair, blue eyes, and fair complexion. We are told she was neat, thoughtful, hard-working, and "never addicted to play like other children" — as though play were some kind of weakness. In eighteenth-century Manchester, childhood was a blight to be overcome as soon as possible.

Young Ann's first job was as a cutter of velvet. Later she prepared cotton for the looms and sheared fur for the hat makers. She worked twelve hours a day, on her feet the entire time because no seats were provided for children. On Sundays, like the other children, she helped clean the equipment, hoping not to be injured by the dangerous machinery.

The mill owners apparently suffered not the slightest twinge of conscience from their exploitation of child labor. Robert Southey, the poet laureate of England who visited Manchester in 1808, said the mill supervisor claimed that infinite good resulted from putting little children to work. " 'You see these children, sir,' said he. 'They get their bread almost as soon as they can walk about, and by the time they are seven or eight years old bring in money. There is no idleness amongst us; they come at five in the morning, we allow them half an hour for breakfast and an hour for dinner; they leave work at six and another set relieves them for the night; the wheels never stand still.' "

Growing up in Manchester must have been a nightmare for a girl who was as sensitive as Ann Lee. The weather varied from misty to damp to rainy; the houses were overcrowded and dirty; the streets reeked with animal and human excrement. The only escape available to the workers from their appalling living conditions was drinking, and there was plenty of that.

Beer houses and gin mills, competing for the laborer's money, opened at the earliest hour and stayed open

TESTIMONIES

OF THE

LIFE, CHARACTER, REVELATIONS AND DOCTRINES

OF

OUR EVER BLESSED MOTHER

ANN LEE,

AND THE ELDERS WITH HER;

THROUGH WHOM THE WORD OF ETERNAL LIFE

WAS OPENED IN THIS DAY OF

CHRIST's SECOND APPEARING:

COLLECTED FROM LIVING WITNESSES,

BY ORDER OF THE MINISTRY,
IN UNION WITH THE CHURCH.

The Lord hath created a new thing in the earth,
A woman shall compass a man. *JEREMIAH.*

HANCOCK:

PRINTED BY J. TALLCOTT & J. DEMING, JUNRS.

—◦◦—

1816.

most of the night. One observer wrote, "It is not just adult males who come to the taverns to drug their minds with alcohol. Alas, no. The mother with her wailing baby, the young girl with her sweetheart, the half-clad, ill-fed child, all are jumbled together in those dirty dens of drink."

It is easy to understand how Ann, repelled by the evils around her, developed a habit of retreating into the world of her imagination. "She was a very peculiar child from infancy," wrote Aurelia Mace, in her early Shaker history, *The Aletheia,* "and often told of having visions of supernatural things." This vivid imagination was to play an important part in Ann's future life.

The children of Manchester were spared no details of life, death, or procreation. Ann used the open toilets with the adults and shared the bedroom with her parents. Perhaps this is why, as a young girl, she developed a strong antipathy toward sex. *Testimonies* gives a dramatic picture of Ann's efforts to prevent her mother from having sexual intercourse with her father.

> In early youth Ann Lee had a great abhorrence of the fleshly cohabitation of the sexes, and so great was her sense of its impurity, that she often admonished her mother against it, which, coming to her father's ears, he threatened and actually attempted to whip her; upon which she threw her-self into her mother's arms and clung around her neck to escape his strokes.

Opposite: The title page of the earliest recorded history of Mother Ann's life and teachings. A new edition of this volume, not to be confused with another volume of testimonies published in 1827, was reprinted in 1888. Courtesy of Flo Morse.

Ann Lee's mother, described as "a good woman, able to instruct and guide her," died early. Ann was left to bring up the younger children. She did her best to teach them right from wrong, but it was almost impossible to combat the moral decay of Manchester. She herself might easily have given up and embraced the animal-like existence of the mill workers, had she not found an unexpected source of strength: Ann discovered religion.

The established church, which she had joined as a child, had been utterly meaningless to her. The coldly intellectual Church of England was more concerned with ritual and power than with the plight of the common people who were at the mercy of brutal laws. (The American Sam Adams called the Church of England "the whore of Babylon.")

In those days, 253 offenses were punishable by death. A man could be hanged if he shot a rabbit, cut down a tree, or stole five shillings' worth of property. Even a ten-year-old child could be sentenced to death. Ann Lee was revolted by a church that condoned such "justice."

About this time two powerful religious figures appeared on the horizon, the great English preachers John Wesley and George Whitefield. Through unceasing effort, this pair of zealous evangelists revived personal religion in England. In the face of continuous insults and persecution, they passionately preached the Gospel and aroused the workers to awareness of their rights as children of God. Because the ministers conducted their worship by "rule and method," they were called Methodists.

When the Reverend George Whitefield came to Manchester to preach there was great excitement. Ann

Lee, eager to hear the famous man, joined the throng that crowded around his outdoor pulpit. Because the disapproving Anglican church had closed its doors to him, Whitefield held his revival meetings under the trees. What he had to say about the all-powerful love of God was not new, but his inflammatory preaching and his outdoor church were. In glowing terms, Whitefield described the direct influence the Holy Spirit could have on a person's daily life. Young Ann was deeply affected by his eloquence and by the crowd's emotional, almost hysterical, response. Whitefield showed her the great power an electrifying preacher can generate. It was a lesson Ann Lee never forgot.

As she struggled to find some meaning in her dreary existence, Ann became increasingly absorbed in the worship of God. It was the year 1758 that marked the turning point in her life. Just twenty-two, and working as a cook in the Manchester infirmary — also called the "lunatic hospital" — to escape the mills, Ann attended a series of religious revival meetings led by Jane and James Wardley. From that time on, her life began to change, first gradually, then dramatically.

The Wardleys were poor tailors from a town near Manchester called Bolton-on-the-Moors. Originally, they had been devout Quakers, dedicated to the belief that true religion comes from inward experience. But in 1747, they received a spiritual message — "a further degree of light and power"— that led them to depart from the Society of Friends to form their own more emotional group called the Wardley Society. They developed an expressive kind of worship that seemed to transport people out of the suffering and sorrows of the physical world to an exalted plane in the spiritual world. The Wardleys were strongly influenced by the ecstatic worship of a radical French group, called Camisards, who migrated to Lancashire in 1685, after Protestantism was forbidden in France.

Ann Lee, filled with enthusiasm for the new movement, soon joined the Wardley Society. She found the meetings deeply satisfying. Services would begin in true Quaker fashion with the men and women sitting in silent meditation. Then they would rise, one by one, and confess their sins. Ann was affected by what she heard. Was it possible that her sins, too, might be redeemed by repentance and confession? She had long been suffocated by an overpowering sense of sin because she was unable to meet the total demands of the Christian faith. "Many times when I was about my work," she said later, "I felt my soul overwhelmed with sorrow and I would work as long as I could to keep it concealed, and then run to get out of sight, lest someone should pity me with that pity which God did not."

In addition to open confession, the Wardley services included impassioned preaching, usually by Mother Jane Wardley. In glowing words, she would tell of mystical experiences — heavenly voices, lights in the sky, visions — and describe the New Era that was coming. Mother Jane rivetted the congregation, not only by her apocalyptic eloquence, but by the simple fact she was a woman. A female preacher was unheard of in Manchester, England.

The climax of the meetings came when the worshippers were moved to express their inner feelings, physically. They would start by walking the floor, chanting and singing. Soon they would be shouting, shaking, and dancing. Because of this they were called "Shaking Quakers," a name first used in ridicule but later widely accepted.

Jane and James Wardley proved invaluable to Ann. In them she found parental figures who offered the firm moral and spiritual guidance she had yearned for. Their meetings gave her life a new meaning. The cleansing power of repentance and the acting out of sinful feelings were therapeutic, but there was another facet of the movement that held a strong attraction for her. It was a revolutionary idea, blasphemous some said. Even today, it would be considered radical. In eighteenth-century England, it was unthinkable. The Shaking Quakers believed that Christ was coming again to reign on earth — and his second appearance would be in the form of a woman.

Ann Lee watched Mother Jane lead the meetings, eloquently proclaiming her belief that God was both male and female, that Christ represented the male principle — but the female principle was yet to come. Ann listened intently as Mother Jane read from Jeremiah: "How long wilt thou go about, O thou backsliding daughter? For the Lord hath created a new thing in the earth, a woman shall compass a man."

And Ann Lee wondered, could it be true? *Was it possible the kingdom of God would be brought forth on earth by a woman?*

Chapter Two

Marriage and Misery

*Wives, submit yourselves to your own
husbands, as unto the Lord. For the husband is the head of the wife, even as
Christ is the head of the church. . .
Therefore, as the church is subject unto
Christ, so let the wives be to their husbands in everything.*

— Saint Paul, The Epistle to the Ephesians,
Chapter 5, verses 22–25

In Ann Lee's day, women were possessions. They were
the playthings, the ornaments, or the servants of men. A
few, a very few, managed to achieve their independence. Ann Lee was one of these.

The intelligence of women was held in low
esteem in eighteenth-century England. Lord Chester-
field, that urbane man of letters, was probably speaking
for most of his countrymen when he wrote, "Women
are to be talked to as below men and above children."

A woman had no legal existence apart from her
husband. A woman could not vote, sign contracts, or
own property. Married women had no title to their own
earnings or even, in the event of legal separation, to
their own children. Few women went to school and
none went to university. It was accepted as a fact that a

woman could not take care of herself. If she had no husband, her father or brothers were responsible for her.

Ann's father, like most eighteenth-century fathers, considered marriage essential to his daughter's security. He insisted that she must marry, whether she wanted to or not. Ann was twenty-six years old and the revulsion against sex, which she had expressed so openly in childhood, still plagued her, but her father gave her no choice. He not only compelled her to marry, he even selected her husband — Abraham Standerin (later called Stanley), a blacksmith who may have been his own apprentice.

Today Ann Lee is considered by many to be a morning star of the women's movement, but at that time she was meekly obedient to her father's commands. Hence it was that on Tuesday, January 5, 1762, "Ann Lees, spinster," was married to "Abraham Standerin, blacksmith." Although Ann had belonged to the Wardley's Shaking Quakers for four years, she was married in her father's Anglican church. Because both the bride and the groom were illiterate, they signed the marriage register with X's. Then they moved in with Ann's father.

The legal concept that marriage creates one person, and at the expense of the woman, was established by William Blackstone, the great English jurist who lived at the same time as Ann Lee. Blackstone stated flatly :"The very being or legal existence of the woman is suspended during marriage, or at least incorporated and consolidated into that of the husband." But Ann refused to go along with such an idea. Showing a remarkable independence of spirit, apparently she continued to be known as Ann Lee. There is no record of her ever being called Ann Stanley. Ann's husband was a lusty, good-humored fellow, "kind according to nature," who did not understand his complicated, headstrong wife.

It would be hard to imagine two people who were more different. Ann, we are told, yearned for a higher life and was always looking for "someone to assist her in the pursuit of true holiness." Abraham Stanley is described as "a decent man who liked his beef and his beer, his corner by the fireplace, and his chair at the tavern."

According to *Testimonies*, these two "lived together at her father's house, in peace and harmony, and procured a comfortable living." This must be a rosy overstatement, since the word "peace" simply does not fit the facts. The marriage of Ann and Abraham was stalked by tragedy from the beginning.

It was normal for an eighteenth-century wife to be continuously pregnant and Ann was no exception. In rapid succession, she gave birth to four children. All of her deliveries were difficult and forceps had to be used in the last one, leaving Ann "lying for hours with little appearance of life."

Although she was naturally maternal, nurturing children was not to be her role. Three of her children died when they were babies and the fourth, Elizabeth, died at the age of six. The Cathedral registry records the burial on October 7, 1766, of "Elizabeth, daughter of Abraham Stanley." The mother's name was not important enough to mention.

The deaths of her four children left Ann Lee almost paralyzed by grief and guilt. She had what would now be called a complete nervous breakdown. Her traumatic suffering is described in *A Summary View of the Millennial Church*, that first Shaker history: "The convictions of her youth often returned upon her with great force. . . . She sought deliverance from the bondage of sin, and gave herself no rest, day or night, but often spent whole nights in laboring and crying to God for deliverance from sin."

Night after night, Ann walked the floor in her stocking feet, asking God's help. "Sometimes I went to bed and slept," she said, "but in the morning I could not feel that sense of the Word of God which I did before I slept. This brought me great tribulation. Then I cried to God, and promised him, that if he would give me the same sense that I had before I slept, I would labor all night. This I did many nights."

Her groans and cries lasted far into the night, making the family tremble. Once her agitation was so great that the bed rocked violently and her husband "was glad to leave it."

Surely Ann knew many women who had buried their children. *Half* the children in Manchester's working class died before the age of five. Ignoring that grim fact, Ann Lee tried to find an explanation for her sorrow in her own behavior. As she prayed and mourned, she gradually convinced herself that her unbearable tragedies were God's judgment upon her. She had sinned by permitting her father and Abraham Stanley to persuade her to forsake her true feelings and marry.

Now, more than ever, Ann was appalled by what she called "the great depravity of human nature and the odiousness of sin, especially of the impure and indecent nature of sexual coition." The deaths of her four children convinced her that sex and marriage were the root of all evil, as indeed they must have been for her. She announced her conclusion to all who would listen: sexual sin had caused her catastrophes.

In desperation she turned to the Wardleys for help. We have in Ann's own words a description of her despair and Mother Jane's peculiar solution for her crisis: "I fell under heavy trials and tribulation on account of lodging with my husband and as I looked to the Wardleys for help and counsel, I opened my trials to Jane. She said, 'James and I lodge together but we do not touch each other any more than two babes. You may return and do likewise.' "

What a relief those words must have been to a woman in hysterical torment. Simply by following the instructions of her spiritual advisor, Ann could escape sexual intercourse, which she loathed, and the inevitable pregnancies as well. She adopted Mother Jane's formula literally. To keep from stirring up her husband's affections, Ann avoided their bed "as if it had been made of embers." She said that she denied herself "every gratification of a carnal nature" and was even afraid to close her eyes at night lest she "awake in hell."

And how did Abraham Stanley take his wife's sudden conversion to celibacy? Not quietly. He was deeply devoted to his emotional wife and her departure from his bed infuriated him. He had violent arguments with her, as all their neighbors could testify. When those proved fruitless, he marched over to the cathedral and angrily complained to the clergy about his wife's conduct. The priests tried to help him. They confronted Ann with the Bible, quoting Saint Paul's directive to women: *Wives, submit yourselves to your own husbands, as unto the Lord.*

It was to no avail. Ann was adamant. She had convinced herself that only a total denial of the body could purify her tortured soul. She would never again have sexual relations with her husband. That was final.

The amazing thing is that Abraham Stanley did not leave his wife. Coping with a preaching, praying, celibate wife required more insight than one might expect from an untutored blacksmith — yet he remained faithful. Indeed, his devotion to her seemed to increase. Ann is quoted as saying, "He would have been willing to pass through a flaming fire for my sake, if I would only live in the flesh with him, which I refused to do."

Instead of departing, Abraham Stanley surprised everybody, perhaps even himself. He decided that he, too, would join the Shaking Quakers. Her husband's conversion to Shakerism and to celibacy is the earliest proof we have of the power of Ann Lee.

Chapter Three

She-Preachers

Sir, a woman's preaching is like a dog's walking on his hind legs. It is not done well, but you are surprised to find it done at all.

— Dr. Samuel Johnson (1709–1784)

Mother Jane Wardley was a "prophetess filled with the Holy Spirit" who could enflame a crowd with her passionate preaching. "Amend your lives!" Mother Jane cried. "Repent, for the Kingdom of God is at hand!" And Ann Lee responded with all her heart and soul. Ann, who never did anything halfway, was by now a dedicated celibate, deeply immersed in the Wardley movement and looking to Mother Jane for her soul's salvation.

The fact that a woman was preaching at all inspired Ann Lee. Many forces in eighteenth-century England kept women repressed, but none was more powerful than the church, where Saint Paul's Letter to the Corinthians was used — as it is even in some quarters today — to define a woman's place: *Let your women keep silence in the churches: for it is not permitted unto them to speak. . . . And if they will learn any thing, let them ask their husbands at home: for it is a shame for women to speak in church.*

The revolutionary idea that a woman might actually be allowed to preach seems to have originated with the Quakers. George Fox, founder of the Society of Friends, could not be called a feminist, but he believed that the spirit of God resides within *every* human being. Under Fox's direction, Quaker women were placed in positions of leadership as early as 1670. Some of his followers considered the idea so monstrous that they left the Society of Friends in protest.

The Wardleys wholeheartedly adopted the Quakers' radical acceptance of women. They encouraged women to speak, and Ann Lee, who was to become one of the most effective women preachers of all time, did her first public speaking when she stood up and confessed at their meetings. Confession, that "cleansing river," as it is called in the fifteenth-century morality play *Everyman,* was the wellspring of the Wardley revivals. Mother Jane told Ann she would never reach God unless she could confess her sins and get rid of everything within her that was not "of God." Of course, Mother Jane added, repentance must go hand in hand with confession; without true repentence, confession was of no value whatsoever.

Repentance came easily to Ann; confession did not. True, she had grown up in the Anglican church which, like the Roman Catholic church, considered private confession between parishioner and priest necessary for anyone struggling to lead a Christian life. But the Wardleys demanded "open confession of every known sin" — which was altogether different.

Ann Lee began her public confessions hesitantly, but before long she was pouring out her transgressions. What a welcome release this must have been for a woman riddled with self-inflicted guilt for the deaths of her four children. She threw herself into an emotional account of her "manifold sins and wickednesses" and people listened, spellbound.

"When I confessed my sins," she said later, "I labored to remember the time when and the place where I committed them. And when I had confessed them, I cried to God to know if my confession was accepted; and by crying to God continually I traveled out of my loss."

Thanks to modern psychiatry, we now know a great deal about the healing power of unburdening the heart. But it was two hundred years before Viennese doctors developed the "talking cure" that Ann Lee's torrent of intense confession helped her to "travel out of" her loss toward a new life. As the psychologist and philosopher William James was to explain two centuries later: "For him who confesses, shams are over and realities have begun; he has exteriorized his rottenness."

It was not only impassioned confession that helped Ann. The Wardleys' insistence that their followers give physical expression to their inner turmoil was also therapeutic. During worship some people would enter into trancelike states; others, seeking release from the weight of their sins, would be overcome by twitching, shaking, and jerking. Ann joined in these strange rituals with fervor.

Under the guidance of the Wardleys, a new life began for Ann Lee. Early Shaker history speaks of Jane and James Wardley's "great power over sin" and goes on to say: "By her faithful obedience to her leaders, Ann

Lee was baptized into the same spirit, and, by degrees, attained full knowledge and experience in spiritual things." Before long, Ann was recognized as a strong spokeswoman for the Wardley Society and began to lead meetings herself.

That Ann had a strong talent for communicating her convictions to others is clear. She persuaded her father, her sister, two of her brothers, and her husband to join the Shaking Quakers. For downtrodden people pinched by poverty and hard work, this ecstatic religious movement must have offered new and joyous hope.

As Ann's personal following increased, so did her persecution by the local authorities. They considered her odd, noisy meetings a threat to the established order of the town. Time and again, Ann was insulted and chased from the streets. Any pretext sufficed to get this erratic woman out of the way.

One Sunday morning when Ann and her followers met in her father's house to worship as usual, spies, who had been placed in the streets by the authorities, sounded an alarm and a mob quickly surrounded the Lee house. With the warden leading the way, the crowd burst into the room where services were being held. In a rush of violence, the worshippers were seized, dragged outside, and carted off to Manchester's stone prison. "The dungeons" was a place of horror where prisoners faced brutality, filth, and cruel neglect.

The next morning everyone was released except Ann Lee and her father. They were kept in the dungeons several weeks for "profaning the Sabbath." Abuse did not dishearten Ann; far from it. The more she was mistreated, the more intense her soul-searching and her religious conviction grew. She intended to preach the Gospel and to help others find God, as she was beginning to find him, and nothing was going to stop her.

Unfortunately, detailed information about Ann's life in England is scant. We know for a fact that Ann was twenty-two years old when she joined the Wardley movement, and twenty-six when she married. It was not until she reached the age of thirty-four that her crusade really began. Ann Lee endured nine years of soul-searching and suffering before she felt prepared to assume her life's work. During those years, we are told, she sought God ceaselessly in "watchings, fastings, tears, and incessant prayer."

At times her agony was excruciating. *Testimonies*, comparing her trials to those of Jesus when he was tempted by the Devil in the wilderness, states: "She labored, day and night, for deliverance from the very nature of sin. And under the most severe tribulation of mind, and the most violent temptations and buffetings of the enemy, she was often in such extreme agony of soul as caused the blood to perspire through the pores of her skin. Sometimes for whole nights together, her cries, screeches and groans were such as to fill every soul around her with fear and trembling."

The years of anguish and fasting caused Ann to waste away until she became a mere skeleton. Elder John Hocknell, a member of the Wardley Society who was with her through much of her suffering, testified that after a series of spiritual crises she was incapable of helping herself. Her naturally strong, healthy body became so emaciated that she was as weak as an infant and had to be fed and supported by others.

Occasionally during her long ordeal, much to the awe of her companions, Ann would be miraculously restored to health. It was said her face would then acquire an unearthly beauty and her eyes would glow. During these strange intervals, she resumed her preaching. Her suffering seemed to give her new power and people gathered about her, fascinated. She exhorted and coaxed until many of them made open confession. Some delivered themselves so completely of their sins they would begin to shiver and shake.

"Shake away the past!" Ann shouted. "Don the white cloaks of a new life!" Such hysterical scenes were too much for official Manchester. Again, Ann Lee was arrested and sent to the stone prison by the Irwell River. This time she was charged with "disturbing the peace."

This extraordinary woman met her trials and tribulations with calm acceptance. She believed pain was necessary to the process of coming out of herself into a broader knowledge of God's presence. In the words of the Shaker hymn, Ann Lee was convinced that in order to be saved, "We must fall on the rock and be broken."

Chapter Four

A Woman
Clothed with the Sun

And there appeared a great wonder in heaven, a woman clothed with the sun, and the moon under her feet and upon her head a crown of twelve stars.

— Revelation, Chapter 12, verse 1

People who have had a religious experience say the breakthrough into a higher realm of power brings a feeling of littleness and helplessness. Then a "holy necessity" takes over; new solutions and new patterns are found, and life assumes a new meaning.

This is exactly what happened to Ann Lee while she was in prison. She was thirty-four years old, in the year 1770, when she beheld the vision that marked the birth of Shakerism. She had been seeking God for nine long years but still felt "hedged up on every side." Once more she "cried mightily to God for help." This time her prayers were answered by a blinding apparition.

We know that as a child Ann, like Joan of Arc, had seen visions and heard voices, but her experience in

23

prison was of a different magnitude. According to *A Summary View,* "The most astonishing visions and divine manifestations were presented to her in so clear and striking a manner, that the whole spiritual world seemed displayed before her." In those soul-splitting moments, Ann felt that the cause of all suffering and the mystery of all evil were revealed to her. In one "glorious klang of being" she grasped the meaning of life, and felt herself resonant as a bell.

First she saw Adam and Eve in the Garden of Eden. She watched them defy God and commit the forbidden sexual act. Then she witnessed their expulsion from the garden by an enraged Deity. All at once it became crystal clear to Ann Lee there was one single cause for humanity's separation from God: *sex.*

Her earlier suspicions were confirmed. It was obvious that all the evil in the world sprang from the hotbed of sexual desire. She realized there was only one way for humanity to recover from its lost state. To enter a new age of spirituality, men and women would have to abstain from "all lustful gratification of the flesh." Self-denial by celibacy was the first essential for those who wanted to gain the spiritual strength to reach God. This was the vision Ann Lee would carry in her heart the rest of her days.

During those moments of mystical ecstasy, a strong current vibrated up and down her spine. Then, as all emotion drained away, a sense of release swept over her and her whole being was suffused with inner harmony and peace. She felt that all her sins were forgiven, all her problems solved.

No wonder Ann Lee walked out of that dank prison filled with new power. For her, the years of seeking were over. She was convinced she had found the truth, and the truth had set her free. She felt at one with God.

Skeptics say a mystic is a person who cannot cope with the real world and, therefore, flees to a world of make-believe. Yet few people would deny that altered states of consciousness do occur. At every time in history and every place on the globe overwhelming, indescribable, mind-changing experiences have been recorded. Joan of Arc, Buddha, Saint Paul, Jesus, Mohammed, Thomas Aquinas, all were transported by religious ecstasy, limitless and unbounded. Ecstasy ("the lifting out of self beyond all reason and control") brought each of them rebirth, followed by peace and certainty that lasted a lifetime. And so it was for Ann Lee. No one can account for these experiences. It is impossible to explain the inexplicable.

As soon as Ann was released from jail, she "took up her cross against the carnal gratifications of the flesh." Speaking with fresh eloquence, she described her vision of the Garden of Eden and attacked sex as the source and foundation of all corruption. According to Shaker historians, her exhortations were delivered with "a heart-searching and soul-quickening spirit that seemed to penetrate every secret of the heart."

She told her listeners that if they would utterly surrender their wills to God, all their earth-born lusts would die away and they would know the bliss of Divine intercourse. Transported by her vision, Ann had escaped from all demands of the flesh and found fulfillment in the world of the spirit.

This reborn woman, radiating spiritual strength, dazzled James and Jane Wardley. They proclaimed her head of their society and news of the intense, eloquent leader spread rapidly. Simple country folk, yearning for a kinder, better life, turned to Ann Lee for help. Factory workers, starved for hope, suddenly found their drab lives brightened by this strange woman's incandescent glow.

Intensity itself can be experienced as the sign of a higher, value-filled existence. For these poor people, mired in misery, Ann's exuberance had great power. When she told them they would never know peace until they gave up sex and sought God, they believed her and expected her to lead them to their Savior.

Why should celibacy appear to Ann Lee as the solution for all the ills of the world? Surely, this is a key question in her life. Perhaps the deaths of her four babies left her with a pathological fear of pregnancy that made her reject sex. Celibacy was most certainly the only reliable method of birth control available.

Or she may have been permanently scarred in early childhood by a fear of sex. For poor families in Manchester, privacy was utterly unknown. Most of the children shared a bed with copulating parents and, apparently, were not deeply affected by the experience. It was just part of life. On the other hand, for a child who possessed Ann's heightened sensibilities, that experience might have been traumatic.

We have already seen how, as a little girl, Ann begged her mother to stay away from her father's bed. Given conditions in Toad Lane, Ann's first impressions of sexual intercourse may have been terrifying. Psychologists now tell us that little children are apt to equate what they see, hear, or imagine occurring between their parents in bed with their own aggressive impulses. Deep in Ann's unconscious, a childish fantasy may have persisted that sex is a brutal assault by a man upon a woman.

Whatever the cause, the result is clear. In her vision, Ann had received "a great light concerning the depravity of human nature." She was now convinced that "weakness of the flesh" caused all worldly sin: lust, vanity, sloth, envy, gluttony, greed, blasphemy. She knew her message was not for everyone. Surely, the world's people would go on marrying and begetting children. But Ann Lee believed with certainty that those who yearned for true holiness would have to follow the path of sexual purity.

Despite Ann's conviction that her problems had been solved, they were actually proliferating. Her biggest difficulty still lay with the forces of law and order in Manchester. The more she called upon her followers to shun sexual relationships and purify their lives by open confession of their sins, the more sensational her meetings became. As *A Summary View* states in rather guarded language: "The most hidden abominations were often brought to light, and those secret acts of wickedness, which had been deceitfully covered under . . . were many times brought to view in such a manner as to make every guilty soul fear and tremble."

These lurid revelations of guilt attracted curious crowds who taunted and jeered at the self-proclaimed sinners. As usual, the authorities were quick to take action. An entry in the Manchester town records shows that on July 14, 1772, Ann Lee, her father (who by now was, apparently, under his daughter's spell), and two others were arrested for creating a public nuisance.

They were arraigned before Justice Peter Mainwaring, who conducted hearings at the Mule Inn, where "considerable ale drinking accompanied the proceedings." At the next session of the court, blacksmith

Mother Ann was imprisoned in the House of Correction, Hunts' Bank, shown here in a facsimile of a drawing by Thomas Barritt. From Richard W. Proctor's *Memorials of Manchester Streets* (1874). Courtesy of Flo Morse. Reproduced by permission of the Local History Library, Central Library, St. Peter's Square, Manchester M2 5PD, England.

John Lee and daughter Ann were sentenced to a month in prison.

Repeated sentences did nothing to dim the religious fervor now rampant in the Lee family. Three months later, the constable broke into their Toad Lane house to quell another noisy revival meeting and, the official record states, "apprehend the gang." This time everyone present was fined, and Ann's brother James was carted off to jail.

It is easy to understand why the local authorities considered the Shakers, as they were now called, a threat to the establishment. Shaker membership was increasing and so was their vehemence against the Church of England. Under Ann Lee's leadership, the Shakers repeatedly attacked the established church for indifference to the suffering of its people and for "condoning marriage." On July 20, 1773, *The Manchester*

Mercury reported that Ann, her sister Betty, and two men marched into Christ Church in Manchester and there "willfully and contemptuously, in the time of Divine service, disturbed the congregation then assembled at morning prayers."

This was an act of almost unbelievable daring, especially for the two women, and authorities were shocked. Again, all were arrested. This time they were fined the staggering sum of twenty pounds. Since they could never raise that amount of money, they were packed off to prison yet again. Undaunted, as soon as Ann got out she resumed her inflammatory preaching. There was no limit to her determination to share God's truth as she knew it.

The word *fanatic* comes from the Latin *fanaticus*, which means "to be put into a raging enthusiasm by a deity." Some said Ann's excessive zeal for religion had now reached the feverish point of fanaticism. Fanatics often possess a mysterious fascination, and certainly that was true of Ann Lee. She could throw the repressed people who were attracted to her into orgies of enthusiasm or indignation. All their dammed-up feelings, their anger at the upper classes, their longing for a better life, were released by her magnetic powers.

Soon bizarre tales began to circulate around Manchester about the Shakers. They were accused of weird behavior, not just shouting and shaking but also frenzied dancing, speaking in tongues, and even witchcraft. The public was aroused, as it always is, by fear of the unknown. As the rumors escalated, charges of fanaticism and heresy led to public abuse of Ann Lee and her followers.

With the increase of danger, some of the new members "fell away," but those who remained grew stronger in their convictions and in devotion to their flamboyant leader. *A Summary View* puts it this way:

> The powerful testimony Ann maintained against all sin, together with the wonderful operations of the Spirit of God which prevailed in the meetings of her little society, excited public attention and stirred up the malignant feelings of many, of almost every class and description, to such a degree of enmity that, by formal opposition and tumultuous mobs, open persecution and secret malice, her very life seemed many times in great jeopardy.

Shaker history is filled with Ann Lee's cliff-hanging escapes from her tormentors. Once she was chased by an angry mob that knocked her down with clubs, kicked and reviled her until "a certain nobleman," who was passing by on his horse, stopped and rescued her. Another time she escaped her pursuers by lying all night on the ice of a frozen pond. She was chilled to the bone but because of her "great peace and consolation" did not even take cold. In another crisis, a friendly neighbor saved her from harm by hiding her beneath a pile of wool in an attic.

Through all vicissitudes, Ann never wavered in her conviction that she was protected by Providence. When one of her own brothers, who felt disgraced by her public behavior, tried to punish her, she said God intervened. Here is her account of their remarkable confrontation.

> So he [her brother] brought a staff, about the size of a large broom handle; and came to me while

I was sitting in my chair, and singing by the power of God. He spoke to me; but I felt no liberty to answer.

"Will you not answer me?" said he.

He then beat me over my face and nose, with his staff, till one end of it was much splintered. But I sensibly felt and saw the bright rays of the glory of God, pass between my face and his staff, which shielded off the blows, so that he had to stop and call for drink.

While he was refreshing himself, I cried to God for His healing power. He then turned the other end of his staff, and began to beat me again. While he continued striking, I felt my breath, like healing balsam, streaming from my mouth and nose, which healed me, so that I felt no harm from his stroke, but he was out of breath, like one which had been running a race.

No wonder Ann's followers began to say she had godlike powers. They claimed she was the woman described in the Book of Revelation who was "clothed with the sun and crowned with the stars." That was going too far. "Blasphemy!" cried the authorities — and locked her up again.

This time they were taking no chances with Ann Lee. They put her in solitary confinement in a tiny cell of the stone prison and kept her locked up without food or water for two weeks. When they finally unlocked her door, after fourteen days of total deprivation, they expected to find her dead on the stone floor. But to their surprise, Ann Lee was alive and well. Those who watched her walk out were speechless. They thought they were witnessing a miracle; surely, no one could survive such an ordeal without supernatural intervention.

There had been intervention all right, but it was not supernatural. What her persecutors did not understand was the devotion of Ann's followers. A dedicated youth named James Whittaker, who had been brought up by Ann Lee, somehow found access to her prison door. Each night, at great risk, he slipped into the jail and stealthily pushed the stem of a pipe through the keyhole of her cell; into the bowl of the pipe he poured milk mixed with wine. Ann had survived on the liquid she sipped from that pipe.

The Shakers thought the jailer's inability to keep Ann locked up was symbolic. One of their earliest hymns expresses the idea:

> *We're children of the free woman*
> *We're free'd from the bondage of sin and death.*
> *If we have any bands a-binding on us*
> *We must break them and break them*
> *And burn them up.*

This song, like other Shaker spirituals, was sung without accompaniment and with an insistent, hypnotic rhythm that created the eerie atmosphere of another world.

Chapter Five

The Female Christ

God is our infinite Mother. She will hold us in her arms of blessedness and beauty forever and ever.

— Theodore Parker (1810-1860)

Miracles abound in Shaker history, some with rational explanations, some without. But none is as incredible as the concept, so central to Shaker thought, that Ann Lee was the *female Christ*. This is, surely, the most difficult part of the Ann Lee story to grasp. Even in a time of women's liberation, the words female Christ have shock value. In the eighteenth century, they must have been almost unthinkable.

The astonishing idea of a female divinity seems to have evolved from two sources: Ann's youthful conditioning in the Wardley movement, and her mystical visitations. Jane and James Wardley had instilled in Ann their belief that Jesus' second coming would be in the form of a woman, because they were convinced that God had to be *both* male and female. They said that the Christ spirit which first appeared in a man, Jesus, would eventually reappear, to fulfill the biblical promise of the second coming, in the form of a woman. "Thereby," the Wardleys prophesied, "God would shake the foundations."

It is essential to understand that at no time did the Shakers actually *worship* either Jesus or Ann Lee. Rather, both were held in deep reverence as the first elders of the Millennial Church, phenomenal beings to be loved and emulated.

The very suggestion that the Messiah might have a feminine aspect was incredible in a day when women were kept totally subservient. Most of the women in England were obliged to marry, submit to their husband's commands, bear countless children, and remain always tethered to the home. The rights of women had not advanced one whit since the Tenth Commandment listed a man's wife as one of his possessions, along with his ox and his ass.

Jane and James Wardley rejected all of the prejudice against women. Over and over, they claimed God had a dual nature. On one side was the eternal Father, symbolized by Jesus; on the other was the eternal Mother, symbolized by a holy woman yet to be chosen. Ann Lee reiterated their claims, at length.

After Ann's next arrest, she was taken, not to jail, but to a madhouse, a rat-infested place of horror where the inmates suffered hideous cruelties. It was while she was there that she had an ecstatic experience that convinced her the Wardleys' prediction had finally come true. She was on her knees in her cell, praying to God for help when, suddenly, rays of light broke in upon her and "the glories of heaven" shone about her. *A Summary View* states as a fact: "She saw the Lord Jesus Christ in his glory."

In that sublime moment, Ann claimed that Jesus had conveyed to her astonishing information. He revealed that *she* was his anointed successor on earth. She, Ann Lee, was chosen to carry his Truth to the world — and Jesus would protect her. Henceforth, she was to be the incarnation of the Word of God, the second coming of *Christ as a woman.*

In her mystical ecstasy, Ann was convinced that the spirit of Christ suffused her being. Her identification with him was complete. "I feel the blood of Christ running through my soul and body!" she cried. "I feel him present with me, as sensibly as I feel my hands together. . . . It is not I that speak. It is Christ who dwells in me."

As soon as Ann was released, she told her followers of her incredible visitation. She, Ann Lee of Toad Lane, had been miraculously changed into Ann, The Word of God Made Manifest in The World. The Wardleys were quick to confirm Ann's new role. They announced that Ann Lee was indeed the female Christ they had long awaited. *Testimonies* describes the rivetting effect of Ann's transfiguration on her associates.

When she was released from her imprisonment, and came to reveal to the society these last extraordinary manifestations, so great was the display of divine light with which her soul was filled and so mighty the power of God which accompanied her testimony, and so keen the searching power of her spirit in discovering and bringing to light the hidden works of darkness, that every soul was struck with astonishment and filled with fear and trembling.

They saw at once that the candle of the Lord
was in her hand, and that she was able by the light
thereof, to search every heart, and try every soul
among them. From this time she was received and
acknowledged as the first visible leader of the
church of God upon earth.

What are we to make of a woman who is known
to her followers as the female Christ? When a person
completely identifies herself with her ideal, many
assessments are possible, from total dedication, to wish
fulfillment, to mental aberration, to hallucination, to
insanity. As a rule, people who believe they incorporate
the divine are megalomaniacs gripped by insane ideas
of their own power. This was never the case with Ann
Lee. Throughout her life she remained a modest woman
who refused to exalt herself. She did not seek acclaim;
her followers bestowed it upon her.

Ann Lee's mystical transformation did not cause
her to lose touch with the real world, nor did it alienate
her from her true identity. On the contrary, after she
was hailed as "the female Christ," Ann developed new
strengths. Her personality grew more powerful, and her
effectiveness in her world greatly increased.

Years later, that devout nineteenth-century
Shaker Aurelia Mace explained why it was possible for
the Shakers to accept Ann Lee's incredible title of
female Christ: "To us God is Father *and* Mother and has
been from the beginning. Jesus was an inspired man.
Ann Lee was an inspired woman. Inasmuch as Jesus
became the Christ, so may all be in possession of the
same spirit."

In other words, spiritual perfection is a possibility open to all seekers after God's truth. Ann Lee was

not Christ, nor did she claim to be. She was, rather, completely absorbed into his spirit and therefore became his female counterpart.

Many in Manchester were appalled by this startling new aspect of Ann's crusade. She had made enemies by asking people to desert their families and join a celibate sisterhood and brotherhood. That was bad enough. But when she described the closeness of her bond with her Savior by saying, "It is not I that speak; it is Christ who dwells in me," the good burghers of the town were horrified.

The more they protested, the more extravagant her rhetoric became. *Testimonies* says she announced: "I have been in fine vallies with Christ as a lover. I am married to the Lord Jesus Christ. He is my head and my husband, and I have no other! I have walked, hand and hand, with him in heaven." Ann's total acceptance of the in-dwelling presence of the Christ spirit was by now complete.

"Blasphemy!" cried the Manchester authorities. This time when they arrested her they threatened to brand her on the cheek and bore through her tongue with a hot poker. They dragged her before a tribunal of four ministers of the established church "with a view to obtain judgment against her." But the judges, who must have been remarkably even-handed, asked Ann Lee to speak for herself.

Speaking was Ann's forte. According to one legend, she spoke to them in twelve languages, including Greek, Latin, Hebrew, and French. In another version, she spoke in seventy-two different tongues. Regardless of these fantastic tales, Shaker history states as a fact that "Mother Ann spoke, and manifested such evident power of God, that they thought proper to dismiss her;

and admonished her accusers to let her alone and not abuse her."

Testimonies describes in chilling terms what happened to Ann after that:

> Enraged and disappointed at not being able to enlist these ministers against her, her persecutors were determined to take the power of judgment into their own hands, and became at once her judges and executioners, and agreed to stone her as a blasphemer. Accordingly they led her down into a valley, without the town, where she was followed by four of her brethren, namely, William Lee, James Whittaker, Daniel Whittaker, and James Shepard.
>
> Her persecutors having provided themselves with a sufficient quantity of stones, suitable for their purpose, they placed themselves on the side of the hill, at a convenient distance, and began to throw their stones; but not being able, after repeated trials, to hit her or any of her companions [except Daniel Whittaker, who received a slight wound on one of his temples], they fell into contention among themselves, and finally abandoned their design.

One might suppose that a woman in danger of being stoned to death would be filled with rage and fear. Not Ann Lee. According to legend, she said afterward: "While they were throwing their stones, I felt myself surrounded with the presence of God, and my soul was filled with love. I knew they could not kill me, because my work was not done; therefore I felt joyful and comfortable, while my enemies felt distress and confusion."

After this crisis, oddly enough, persecution of the Shakers in Manchester seemed to abate. Perhaps Ann Lee and her followers became more circumspect about conducting their exuberant worship — "singing and dancing, shaking and shouting, speaking with new tongues and prophesying" — in public. Or perhaps Ann's enemies were intimidated because, as *Testimonies* states with simple faith: "They saw that she was evidently protected and supported, and her life preserved, by some interposing power." Whatever the reason, Ann Lee and her little band were, for a time, allowed to pursue their religion in peace.

Mother Ann, as she was called from then on, "always stood ready to obey the call of God." She did not relax when her life grew calmer. Quite the contrary. It was at this juncture that she embarked on the most ambitious project of her entire life.

News of the English colonies in America had filtered back to Toad Lane. It was rumored that freedom, especially freedom from coercion, was so vital to the Americans that they were ready to fight the British for it. Mother Ann's active imagination was stimulated by what she heard. Of course, fighting was anathema to all Shakers, but they yearned for freedom. How wonderful it would be to escape from a world where a person could be put to death for "unacceptable" religious convictions.

After the Reverend George Whitefield returned from his fifth trip to America, he again came to Manchester to preach. With blazing eloquence, Whitefield described the opportunities for a rebirth of the spirit in America. Mother Ann, who had never been out of Manchester, was deeply impressed by Whitefield's descriptions of the New World. She began to think seriously of going there.

When Mother Ann meditated on a subject, mystical revelations often followed. This time she had a vision that the true church was to be established in America. She "saw" that the colonies would one day gain their independence, and then freedom of conscience would be secured for all people to worship God without "hinderance or molestation." Mother Ann said she saw a chosen people waiting for her in New England and she knew then that God wanted her to take the Millennial Church to America and that he would aid her in this enormous undertaking.

Other members of the Society had signs and visions that confirmed Mother Ann's daring idea. One night, when a little group of Believers was resting by the roadside after a twenty-mile walk, a mysterious vision appeared to young James Whittaker. He saw a large tree "whose leaves," he said, "shone with such a brightness as made it appear like a burning torch." Whittaker took this to mean that he was to help plant the tree of faith in the new world. Mother Ann never forgot his image of the shining tree of faith, and she later adopted it as a Shaker symbol.

A meeting was called to discuss the possibility of a trip to America. One after another, the Shakers rose to testify to the divine summons. Ann Lee said of that fateful evening: "There were so many gifts in confirmation of our going — such as prophecies, revelations, visions, and dreams — that some could hardly wait for others to tell their gifts and we had a joyful meeting and danced till morning."

And so the mission to the New World was set. Mother Ann would lead it, accompanied by those members of the society "who felt any special impressions on their own minds so to do." Despite all of the early enthusiasm, only eight Shakers had the determination and fortitude needed for this journey into the unknown. They were Abraham Stanley, her husband; William Lee, her brother; Nancy Lee, her niece; John Hocknell, with his son Richard; James Whittaker, Mary Partington, and James Shepard. Three were members of Ann's own family. It is remarkable that her much abused husband elected to go with her. He must have decided a celibate marriage was preferable to a life without his vibrant wife.

Even the intrepid Mother Ann was apprehensive about the dangers that lay ahead. She said, "I know fresh scenes of trial and bitter persecutions await me in America, still my obedience to the Call gives me power to comply." The others were fearful, too, but they placed their trust in Mother Ann. One proof of her power as a leader is the fact that after she left England, the Shakers dwindled away to nothing. From then on, Shakerism was to be a purely American phenomenon. It seems unbelievable that a simple, uneducated woman could lead such a dangerous venture into unknown realms.

Ann Lee might easily have succumbed to the hopelessness that suffocated men and women in the Manchester slums. Instead, burdened by poverty and ignorance though she was, she somehow managed to pull together this small band of followers to seek a new life in a new world where, eventually, they would leave their mark. How, one must ask, could such a thing happen?

Leila Taylor and Anna White, in their book *Shakerism: Its Meaning and Message,* pose this question and give the Shakers' answer: "Why was Ann Lee so unlike the other poor women of Manchester, her neighbors in Toad Lane? Because she listened for the voice of God and obeyed his call."

Chapter Six

The New World

Put your hands to work and your hearts to God.

— Mother Ann Lee

After the great decision to transport the Shaker faith to America, excitement ran high. It was a prodigious undertaking, but Mother Ann and her eight disciples were excited by the challenge. She commissioned John Hocknell to look for a ship whose passage they could afford. Hocknell was the right one to send. He was the only one of the group who had any money and he apparently financed the others. Without his help, the Shakers would never have left England.

Although most of the Believers were poor, they were lucky enough to find two well-to-do sponsors at critical moments in their early history. The first was John Townley, a wealthy Manchester builder who, at the very beginning of the movement, invited the controversial Wardleys to live in his home on Canon Street and conduct their meetings under his protection. The second was Townley's brother-in-law, this same John Hocknell who sponsored the American voyage.

Hocknell, a man of property from Cheshire, was so enthusiastic about the Shaker ideal of communal living that he invited some of the impoverished members to move into his house. His wife, Hannah, was infuriated. She and her brothers, who were described as "high-spirited people," had him arrested and put in jail. But after Hocknell was tried and released, Hannah, whose anger must have been fleeting, announced that she was going to join the Society of Believers herself. Although Sister Hannah Hocknell became a devout Shaker, she refused to go along with her husband and their son Richard when they decided to make the hazardous journey to America.

Brother Hocknell managed to book inexpensive passage for the nine Shakers aboard the sailing ship *Mariah*. He felt compelled, however, to tell Ann Lee why it was cheaper than the other ships. The *Mariah* had been condemned. This bad news did not dismay the imperturbable Mother Ann. "God would not condemn it," she said, "while we are on it."

When the skipper of the ship, Captain Smith, saw his unusual passengers, he must have had some misgivings. Ann Lee was quick to reassure him. *A Summary View* says: "Before they embarked, Mother Ann told the captain that he would not have whereof to accuse them, except it were concerning the law of their God." This turned out to be literally true.

It is almost impossible for a person accustomed to the speed and comfort of twentieth-century travel to imagine a voyage across the Atlantic Ocean in 1774. The tiny wooden ships were stinking and unventilated; the unrefrigerated food was nearly inedible; the bathing and toilet facilities were almost nonexistent. Unreliable maps, unpredictable winds and weather, and a total lack of communication with the outside world made for a lengthy, dangerous trip.

The *Mariah* sailed out of Liverpool on May 19, 1774, on a spring tide with the brave little band of Shakers aboard. A wave of relief must have washed over them as they looked for the last time upon England. They were escaping from cruel and continuous persecution. Full of hope, they turned their thoughts toward the New World where, they had been told, religious freedom was the right of every human being.

It is easy to visualize Ann Lee standing resolutely at the ship's rail in her blue-and-white checked dress. We know that is what she wore on the trip because a swatch of the cotton material has been preserved and is now on display at the Shaker Museum in Chatham, New York, along with a flower-bordered teacup and saucer she is said to have brought with her, fragile eighteenth-century relics of a rugged pilgrimage.

The *Mariah* usually took three months to cross the Atlantic, longer if the weather was bad. Mother Ann Lee knew how to make use of the time. As soon as the ship was riding the waves, she began organizing religious services. Each day the Shakers spent hours worshipping in their unorthodox fashion. At first, the sailors were entertained by the praying, preaching, singing, dancing, and shouting of their peculiar passengers. But when Mother Ann began to pour her preaching talents into testifying against the wickedness of the crew, they protested.

Captain Smith ordered all services stopped at once. Mother Ann ignored him. She continued to pray loudly for the men of the *Mariah*. The captain, used to obedience on board his ship, was enraged. He threatened to put all the Shakers in irons, and if that did not stop the preaching and praying, he vowed he would have them cast into the sea. Mother Ann feared God far more than she feared Captain Smith. The next day she conducted worship as usual, with special prayers for all seafaring sinners. The captain, shouting with anger, again threatened to have them thrown overboard. But before any action could be taken, fate — and Mother Ann — intervened. *A Summary View* describes the emergency in dramatic terms.

It was in the evening, in the time of a storm; and the ship suddenly sprung a leak, occasioned by the starting of a plank between wind and water. The water now flowed in so rapidly, that notwithstanding all their exertions at the pumps, it gained upon them so fast that the whole ship's crew were greatly alarmed. The captain turned pale as a corpse, and said they must all perish before morning, for he saw no possible means to save the ship from sinking.

Mother Ann said, "Captain, be of good cheer. There shall not a hair of our heads perish. We shall all arrive safe to America. I just now saw two bright angels of God standing by the mast, through whom I received this promise."

She then encouraged the seamen, and she and her companions zealously assisted at the pumps. Shortly after this, a large wave struck the ship with great violence, and the loose plank was instantly closed to its place.

Whether this remarkable incident was effected by the violent force of the wave against the plank, or by some other unaccountable means, it was then viewed by all on board as a miraculous interposition of Divine Providence in their favor.

The Believers were soon in a great measure released from the pumps; and the captain after this, gave them free and full liberty to worship God according to the dictates of their own consciences, and promised that he would never molest them again. He was faithful to his promise, and treated them with kindness and respect during the remainder of the voyage, and declared afterwards that had it not been for these people, he should have been sunk in the sea, and never reached America.

Running through this story of supernatural rescue at sea are two golden threads woven into the fabric of all Shaker history: faith in God and zest for hard work. Ann Lee did not rely on the promise of help from the two bright angels; she manned the pumps as well. Linking hard work to devout worship was a vital aspect of Shaker belief. *Put your hands to work and your hearts to God.* That was the motto of Mother Ann's life, and the firm foundation on which she built the Shaker movement.

During their seventy-nine days at sea, the Shakers had ample time to discuss how they were going to cope with the problems ahead of them. Their future was in every way uncertain. They had no idea where they would live, nor how they would find work, nor where they might establish their religious community. But they had faith that God would unfold these things for them. In their wildest dreams, they never could have imagined what would prove to be one of the biggest difficulties they would encounter in the New World: the Revolutionary War.

An early Shaker hymn, "Voyage to Canaan," although clearly symbolic (sin is referred to as "that dreadful ocean"), seems to recall the end of the Believers' epic voyage across the Atlantic on the *Mariah*.

> *The passengers united*
> *In order peace and love;*
> *The wind all in our favour,*
> *How sweetly we do move!*
> *Let tempests now assail us,*
> *And raging billows roar,*
> *We will sweep thro' the deep,*
> *Till we reach the blessed shore.*

On August 6, 1774, the *Mariah* finally sailed into New York harbor. What a vast relief for all on board! After a perilous crossing on a crowded, leaking, condemned ship, they must have been worn out. One can imagine the mixture of thanksgiving, excitement, fatigue, and anxiety that gripped the travelers when at last the eight church steeples of old New York appeared on the horizon.

Dauntless as ever, Mother Ann led her little band ashore. They were poor English immigrants in a strange land where people were turning against the English. They had no friends in America and no immediate means of support. But they did have something they had not known in the squalor of Manchester. They had hope.

New York City was very different from the smoky factory town where Ann Lee was born. It was a pleasant town filled with trees and gardens. Most New

Yorkers lived below Wall Street. North of Washington Square were farmhouses, grazing cattle, and country lanes. Down Fifth Avenue from Twenty-first Street flowed a sparkling brook where trout could be caught, while the shooting of duck and quail abounded along the banks of the Hudson.

But in many ways New York was becoming sophisticated. With a population of twenty thousand, it was the third-largest city in the colonies, after Boston and Philadelphia. King's College (later Columbia University), the New York Hospital, and the Public Library had already been established. Under British rule, the city had acquired streetlights, a postal service, a newspaper, and a fire department, as well as prisons and poorhouses. One thing that was new to the Shakers — and horrifying — was the public slave market where black men, women, and children were sold from an auction block. To Mother Ann, who *knew* that every human being was a child of God, the slave trade was as sinful as it was incomprehensible.

On that quiet Sunday afternoon in August, the nine Believers walked up "Broad Way" and turned into Queen Street (now Pearl Street) looking for lodgings. According to Shaker history, they stopped at a building occupied by a family named Cunningham. The mistress of the house was sitting outside to escape the heat. She must have been dumbfounded when Mother Ann stepped up to her, called her by name, and made the startling announcement: "I am commissioned by the Almighty God to preach the everlasting gospel to America, and an Angel commanded me to this house and to make a home for me and my people."

There is no record of Mrs. Cunningham's reply. Apparently, she was moved by the conviction and the

magnetism of the strange visitor, because the Cunningham family welcomed the travelers, and Ann and her
husband moved in with them. By happy coincidence,
Mr. Cunningham was a blacksmith and Abraham
Stanley was able to work in his smithy.

Testimonies adds these touching details: "Mother
Ann employed herself in washing and ironing for her
living, and by her meekness, humility, and amiable
deportment, she gained the love and esteem of the
woman of the house by whom she was treated with
great kindness." Ann Lee and Abraham Stanley
remained with their new friends the Cunninghams for
over a year.

The other Shakers also found menial jobs
and places to board. All believed their meager living arrangements were temporary. Mother Ann
had promised them that if they endured their
present poverty and suffering without turning
away from God, he would reward them in the future. If
their trust in Mother's word ever wavered, they kept it
quiet. Repeatedly, she charged them to seek God's
guidance. "God's world must be learned," she said,
"much as a trade is learned. You have to work at it.
God's grace can give us faith, but we must be as
simple as a child to make that faith our own and to live
by it."

In America, as in England, Ann Lee's life was
entirely God-centered. Everything else was secondary,
including her husband. She continued to believe that
the true source of human corruption was sex. No one
could reach God, she declared, while wallowing in the
lust of the flesh. Abraham Stanley, having endured her
sexual abstinence for six years, began to spend his
nights drinking. When he was drunk, he shouted and

cursed Ann for adopting a crazy religion that made her refuse to sleep with her husband.

Mother Ann tried to explain to him that her natural instincts had died away in love of God, but the more she talked of "the exuberant bliss of Divine intercourse," the more Abraham drank. Ann, deeply absorbed in her spiritual journey, bore her husband's intoxicated abuse with patience. But their "marriage" was becoming intolerable. In dramatic detail, *A Summary View* describes the turning point in their peculiar relationship.

Abraham Stanley was visited with a severe sickness. To nurse and take care of him required Mother Ann's whole time and attention. This duty she performed with the utmost care and kindness, tho often at the expense of great sufferings on her part. Their earnings now ceased, and they were reduced to extreme poverty.

Abraham at length recovered his health, so as to be able to walk the streets; and tho he never had been considered as a faithful and substantial Believer; yet he had hitherto supported his credit and reputation, and maintained an outward conformity to his faith.

But on regaining his health, and before he was fully able to return to his occupation, he began to associate with the wicked at public houses, and soon lost all sense and feeling of religion, and began to oppose Mother Ann's testimony in a very ungodly manner, and urged her to renounce it, and live in sexual cohabitation, like the rest of the world.

She replied, that she was willing to do any

thing for him which justice, reason, or humanity required; but she should never consent to violate her duty to God; and endeavored to prevail on him to return to his duty and be faithful.

But as Abraham was determined to pursue the course of the world, he continued his vicious practice, instead of returning to his occupation, and left Ann to provide for herself. At length he brought a lewd woman into the house to her, and declared that, unless she would consent to live in sexual cohabitation with him, he would take that woman for his wife.

Ann replied with great firmness and resolution, that she would not do it if he should take her life as a consequence of her refusal. She also informed him in plain terms, that she considered his cruel and abusive conduct as a very unjust requital for the uniform kindness and attention which she had paid to him, both in sickness and in health; and she said she was still willing to take the most tender care of him, if he would return to his duty, and conduct himself as he ought to do, and urged him, in the most feeling manner, to return to the obedience of his faith; but all to no effect.

He soon went off with the woman, to a distant part of the city, and it was reported that he was shortly after married to her.

Thus ended Ann Lee's thirteen years of marriage to Abraham Stanley. Exactly how the bonds of matrimony were dissolved we have no way of knowing. But we do know from then on she was thrown entirely upon her own resources, a dire situation for a woman in the eighteenth century.

During that long, bitter winter Mother Ann endured "deep sorrow of the soul." Her children were dead. Her husband had left her. Her mission to America seemed doomed. Despite repeated declarations of her faith in God's help, the chilling fact remained that she and her little band of followers were staggered by poverty, privation, even hunger. In those bleak days she tasted the bitterness of despair.

Testimonies, describing Mother Ann's plight, paints a doleful picture of her praying in a barren room with "a cold stone for a seat, and her only morsel a cruse of vinegar." Then come these touching words: "Mother Ann sat down upon the stone, without any fire, sipped her vinegar and wept."

Chapter Seven

Escape to the Wilderness

And to the woman were given two wings of a great eagle that she might fly into the wilderness.

— Revelation, Chapter 12, verse 14

Mother Ann did not stay bogged down in despair; her nature was too buoyant for that. One of her colorful comments, preserved in the records of her followers, was addressed to a man steeped in self-pity. "Hold up your head," she told him. "God made man upright. Don't lean against walls. You walk crooked. Be cheerful! Be cheerful!"

With that same spirit Ann Lee pulled herself together after her husband's departure. She would not think about her own troubles. She would concentrate on the immense, seemingly impossible, task of establishing the Shaker faith in America.

It was the worst of times for such a venture. The Believers had accomplished nothing in the year they had spent in this country and now war was closing in on them. The summer of 1775 was turbulent in New York City. Patriots were inflamed by the Battle for Bunker Hill fought in Boston that June, a victory for the British — but what a victory! King George III could not afford to subdue many more American "farmers" at such a cost.

Acts of violence against the hated British Tories were increasing throughout the colonies. In New York, a troop of Americans rode to the shop of a Loyalist printer, smashed his presses, and carried off his type. Tories were persecuted, and in one instance a Tory woman was carried about on a rail by patriot women. A resolution passed by the Town Meeting in Boston told the story: "The whole United Colonies are upon the verge of a glorious revolution. We have seen petitions to the king rejected with disdain. For the prayer of peace, he has tendered the sword; for liberty, chains; for safety, death. Loyalty to him is now treason to our country."

Treason is a dire word. Clearly, these were dangerous days for a tiny band of British pacifists struggling to bring forth God's kingdom in America. Mother Ann realized her only hope was to gather her scattered group and leave New York. As *A Summary View* put it: "Religious freedom was dearer to her than life." She was determined to achieve that freedom for her people at all costs.

Once again, Mother Ann turned to John Hocknell for help. He agreed that a move was urgent. He had a little money left and had heard that land was cheap in the upstate town of Albany, so he boarded a sloop and sailed up the river to investigate.

Although everything outside Albany except the tiny hamlet of Schenectady was wilderness and Indians, Albany itself was a charming settlement built on three hills overlooking the beautiful Hudson River. Hocknell liked it at once and was sorely disappointed when he could find no land affordable to him. Then, according to Shaker legend, a most peculiar thing happened. He was praying for guidance when, suddenly, his arm rose of its own accord and his finger pointed toward the northwest. Following this strange lead, he went in that direction to see what he could find.

Whether or not this odd event actually occurred, the fact is that Hocknell did discover a promising tract of woods eight miles northwest of Albany. Since it was remote property belonging to a wealthy patroon named Stephen Van Rennsselaer, he hoped he could purchase it with ease. John Hocknell, devout Shaker, must have been awed when he called on the Lord of the Manor Rensselaerwyck in his elegant brick home beneath the drooping elms. Van Rensselaer, like the other patroons, had received his huge estate from the Dutch when they owned New York, and his manor house, built as a gift for his bride, was considered one of the handsomest residences in the colonies.

Squire Van Rensselaer listened to Hocknell with interest. No, he would not sell that wilderness property — christened Niskeyuna by the Indians — but he agreed to lease it to the Shakers "in perpetuity." Many references say Niskeyuna means "Good Corn Land," which is incorrect. It means "Where the Water Flows." In the eighteenth century, the property included a winding river, now reduced to a choked stream. The area was called Watervliet by the Dutch. Later it was given the "spiritual name" Wisdom Valley by the Shakers.

A jubilant Hocknell returned to New York to tell Mother Ann about the land he had leased for the

Shakers. She was elated — especially when he described the isolation of Niskeyuna. At long last, the Believers were going to find security in seclusion. Now God would make their dream come true. Withdrawing from the world into a community of their own, they would be able to establish the Millennial Church. It was an incredibly ambitious undertaking.

Mother Ann wanted to move to Niskeyuna at once, but John Hocknell said that was impossible. First, he must return to England to get his wife and the rest of his family and, he added, "make further arrangements for the settlement of the Society in this country." In plain words, that meant raising more money. Ann's brother William Lee, who had found work as a blacksmith, and James Whittaker, now employed as a weaver, offered to contribute all the cash they could earn for the move to Niskeyuna, but much more was needed.

One can only marvel at Hocknell's energy and dedication. He made the long journey back to England, sold all his property, packed up his ex-Methodist family, and made the dangerous trip back to America to join a struggling religious group on a pilgrimage into the wilderness. At that time, John Hocknell was seventy years old.

While Hocknell was away, William Lee and James Whittaker spent all their spare time on the backbreaking task of clearing the newly acquired land. An impatient Mother Ann made several journeys up the river that autumn to inspect Niskeyuna and urge them to make haste. The sooner the Shakers could leave New York City, the better. They could already feel the hot breath of Revolution on their necks.

Christmas day, 1775, John Hocknell and his family landed in Philadelphia, bringing the John Partington family with them to join the Shaker adventure. They proceeded to New York City by land and went at once to Mother Ann, who welcomed them with open arms. Now she and her disciples could finally begin the big move to Niskeyuna. All had remained faithful to Mother except her rebellious husband, Abraham Stanley, "who was heard of no more."

To go from New York to Albany in those days, you consulted not a timetable but a calendar. In mild weather, you took a boat, but when the Hudson was frozen, you went by stagecoach. Either way, it was a three-day trip. Because the Shakers had to transport all of their supplies, they decided on the boat. Soon after the ice left the river, they boarded a sloop bound for Albany.

They got out of New York just in time. Had they lingered, they would have been embroiled in war. During the summer of 1776, American patriots were on the rampage. Nothing British was safe. When a copy of the Declaration of Independence arrived from Philadelphia, General Washington ordered it read aloud at evening parade and New Yorkers went wild. In the hysteria, a mob threw a rope around the statue of King George III and tugged it down. In a nice bit of symbolism, the lead from his statue was later converted into anti-British bullets by the women of Litchfield, Connecticut.

That August, twenty-five thousand English soldiers led by General Howe landed in New York. They were backed up by a powerful fleet under his brother, Lord Howe. The Howes forced George Washington, who had only eight thousand men, to abandon the city. Not long afterward, English frigates sailed into the Hudson. For the next seven years, New York City belonged to the British.

By conquering and holding the entrance to the Hudson River, the British hoped to cut the United Colonies in two and thus defeat them. To the Tories, the British army and navy were the king's righteous answer to the traitorous Declaration of Independence. To the Shakers, both the American and the British fighters were sinners desecrating God's supreme law — "love thy neighbor as thyself."

It is easy to imagine how happy the Believers were to leave the turmoil of the warring city behind. Once more filled with hope, they stood on deck as their sloop sailed slowly past the Palisade cliffs, the wild, wooded shores of Westchester, and the awesome Storm King Mountain. Their childlike trust in God gave them the kind of optimism that was expressed in the first Shaker hymn, "The Happy Journey."

The heavens of glory is our destination
We're swiftly advancing to that happy shore;
We're travelling on in regeneration,
And when we get through we shall sorrow no more.

This beautiful journey which we've undertaken,
Excels all the travel that ever has been,
And those that perform it will never be shaken,
Because it leads out of the nature of sin.

Chapter Eight

"Good Woman"

*Do all your work as though you had a
thousand years to live; and as you would
if you knew you must die tomorrow.*

— Mother Ann Lee

When Mother Ann opened the first colony at Niskeyuna in 1776 she was forty. A short woman with proud bearing and penetrating blue eyes, her hard life had made her strong. She was able to work long hours with the men, clearing and draining the land, building cabins with crude tools, and planting crops under the burning sun. Like all true leaders, Mother Ann never asked her people to do anything she would not do herself.

The first months were frightening. Food was scarce; insects and snakes from the nearby swamp plagued the settlers; sickness and fever were rampant. Mother Ann nursed the sick and heartened the discouraged. Nothing could dim her enthusiasm because at last she had found a sanctuary for her people. *A Summary View* describes the situation: "The place being then in a wilderness state, they began, with indefatigable zeal and industry, and through additional sufferings, to prepare the way for a permanent settlement, where they could enjoy their faith in peace, amid the tumults of the war in which the country was then involved."

The Shakers were in no way retreating from reality when they settled at Niskeyuna. The hardships they endured in their struggle to establish a Utopian community on the edge of civilization would have defeated them had they been dreamers and not doers. Their very survival was in question. Of the many dangers they faced — scarcity of food, exposure to bad weather, illness, wild animals — the most threatening may have been the Indians. The immigrants from Manchester had never seen an Indian before. Naturally, they were afraid of their nearest neighbors, the Mahicans. Known also as River Indians, the Mahicans were part of the Algonkian race. Once they had owned Albany and they resented all white intruders.

Mother Ann heard that the Mahicans (the name means "wolf") had beaten the Mohawks, killing and scalping them. Then, after applying to the governor for free rum "to comfort our hearts," they demolished the French. It took courage for her to approach them. But having dedicated her life to living in love and charity with her neighbors, she was not going to be put off by the mere fact that her neighbors happened to be murderers. Just as any housewife would do in England, Mother Ann put on her bonnet and went to call on the people next door.

The Mahicans must have been surprised when the energetic little woman with the blue eyes and warm smile arrived at their tepee camp. Mother Ann was the kind of person who made an impression. *A Summary*

View reports, "Her manners were plain, simple, and easy, and she possessed a certain dignity of appearance that inspired confidence and commanded respect."

If only we knew more details of her confrontation with the Mahicans! It must have been a colorful scene. Shaker legend claims that her "gift of tongues" enabled her to converse with the Indians in their own dialect. However that may be, the meeting ended with Mother Ann sitting on the ground, smoking the peace pipe with her ferocious neighbors.

According to the Shakers, the Indians were the first to realize there was something strange about the leader of the little colony in the woods. One of the braves announced that he saw a "bright light" surrounding Mother Ann. "The Great Spirit has sent this woman to do much good," he declared. From then on, the Mahicans honored Mother Ann with the title "Good Woman."

"Good Woman's" friendship with her neighbors turned out to be crucial. The Shakers never could have survived their first year in the wilderness without the help of the Indians. The Mahicans brought gifts of food and taught them many things, from growing corn to tapping maples for syrup. They showed them how to dry seeds and weave baskets, make herbal medicines and dyes — skills the Shakers would later develop into fine arts.

And when the white "wolf moon," as the Indians called the full moon of January, glittered over the frozen countryside, it was the Mahicans who showed the Shakers how to fish through ice and track wild animals for food. Most valuable of all, they taught the gentle people from England ways to protect themselves from the bone-chilling, below-zero weather.

No matter what hardships Mother Ann and her followers faced, memories of their escape from Manchester must have made the New World seem promising. One of Mother Ann's famous contemporaries, twenty years her senior, was the poet and artist William Blake. Like Mother Ann, Blake was deeply and unconventionally religious. It was his cry of indignation that later drew the world's attention to "the dark Satanic mills of Manchester," which Ann had fled.

To Mother Ann, the wilderness was congenial. She had already journeyed during those soul-searching years in England, to a much more frightening space — the wilderness within. Miraculously, she had discovered there the Christ spirit. She told her people over and over that they, too, must go down into their own interior spaces to find the gentleness of Christ which lay within each of them. Only by making that inward journey could they prepare for the hardships that life was sure to bring.

Mother Ann never doubted that the little Shaker settlement at Niskeyuna would eventually flourish, but some of the others were not so sure. To sustain their sagging morale, and to get the utmost out of every day, she required all Believers to follow a strict schedule. She knew instinctively that rigorous discipline can be supportive to people living in a strange environment. Discipline gives life a reliable framework, freeing the mind for other things.

Mother Ann's daily regime left no time for self-pity, self-doubt, or self-indulgence. The Shakers rose at daylight and worked continuously until dark, stopping at regular intervals to worship God and rejoice in the opportunity he had given them. Mother Ann's evening prayer sessions, attended by weary men and women after a long day's labor, were never thought of as a "duty" but were anticipated with pleasure and enjoyed as refreshment.

This is an important difference between the Shakers and their Puritan contemporaries. Both sects practiced the virtues of simplicity, austerity, hard work, and denial of the flesh, not for personal gain but for the glory of God. Both believed self-denial had meaning only as it contributed to the salvation of the soul. But the early Shakers relished life, while the Puritans permitted themselves little pleasure.

Since Shakers and Puritans alike thought the world might end at any moment, they lived in constant awareness of their souls. The purpose of life was to prepare to meet one's maker face-to-face. As Mother Ann said in one of her most quoted remarks, "Do all your work as though you had a thousand years to live, and as you would if you knew you must die tomorrow."

While the Puritans valued thought and suppressed feeling, the Shakers exalted feeling, so long as it was not sexual in nature. This is a paradox, since Puritans married and had children while Shakers, sworn to celibacy, rejected sex as the primary cause of sinfulness. The difference seems to lie in the word joy. For Puritans were suspicious of joy. Mother Ann insisted joy was the elixir of life.

Puritans were forbidden to dance and sing. Shakers relished both. Their songs and dances, highly charged with emotion, were essential, not only as a way to worship God, but also for recreation and release from tension. Mother Ann must be given credit for Shakerism's early emphasis on jubilation. She declared that dancing and singing were mysterious gifts from God that promoted unity among people of all kinds.

In the beginning, Shaker dancing and singing were formless. Both were done without any instrumental accompaniment. The impulsive whirlings and discordant shoutings later gave way to rhythmic chants, "step songs," "square order shuffles," and hymns of praise and thanksgiving. In dancing, as in everything else, Shakers never mingled the sexes. Males and females faced each other in straight lines, advancing and retreating, marching and circling, but never, never touching. One of the earliest of the "Millennial Praises" expresses their simple joy in being together:

> *We love to dance, we love to sing,*
> *We love to taste the living spring,*
> *We love to feel our union flow,*
> *While round, and round, and round we go.*

God was at all times a powerful presence at Niskeyuna. Mother Ann made sure of that, as is clear in a graphic account of the Shakers' first Christmas in their new community told in a booklet called "The Shaker Order of Christmas," by Edward and Faith Andrews. Since the Believers did not deify Jesus, they were unsure how they should observe Christmas — until Mother Ann "received a sign" through John Hocknell's wife, Hannah. It is a typical Shaker legend.

It was still dark when Hannah Hocknell
awoke on that December morning in 1776. A cold
wind was sweeping over the desolate swamp of
bogs, wild grass, and weeds beside which the cabin
stood, and rattling the branches in the surrounding
forest. The deep slough-holes formed by the mean-
dering Scherluyn Creek were already frozen, and

on this morning Hannah could hear occasional
flurries of sleet pelting against the cabin.

Rising from the husk mattress which served as
a bed, the elderly Shakeress lit a candle, started a
fire, and began to dress in preparation for her usual
day's work. To the world outside the Shaker settlement, it was Christmas morning. But to Hannah, as
one who still followed the old-style Julian calendar,
it was in no wise different from other mornings.
She had sweeping to do, and washing for the family of four sisters and six brethren. After a simple
breakfast of bean porridge and root tea she would
attend to these tasks, faithful to the injunction of
Mother Ann Lee, the foundress of the order, to put
her hands to work and her heart to God.

For some unaccountable reason, however, the
"old Believer" could not lace her shoes: a peculiar
shaking or agitation of the limbs hindered all her
efforts. She was still standing by the stove, bent
over, struggling for control, when Mother Ann herself, lamp in hand, appeared at the doorway.
Watching for a while, the prophetess was finally
moved to speak — from the Scriptures, as was so
often her wont:

"Try no longer, Hannah! Put off thy shoes from
off thy feet, for the place whereon thou standest is
holy ground."

Mother Ann recognized in Hannah's experience a "gift": that this was a holy day on which no
manual labor should be done, a day to be dedicated exclusively to cleaning the house of the spirit.

So originated the Shaker order of Christmas.
Sister Hannah's resolution to do the washing and clean-

ing, and Mother Ann's inspiration as she stood at the door, led to the annual rituals of "The Open Door" and "The Opening of the Mind." From that day forward, Shakers spent the days before Christmas in ceremonial sweeping and scrubbing to commemorate the first Christmas at Niskeyuna. As they scoured, they chanted work songs.

> *Sweep, sweep and cleanse your floor,*
> *Mother's standing at the door,*
> *She'll give us good and precious wheat,*
> *With which there is no chaff nor cheat.*

The cleansing, with real mops and with spiritual brooms, was to wash away all "stains of sin" in preparation for the great Shaker dream — the birth of the Christ spirit in every human heart.

The Believers at Niskeyuna were enlarging their forms of worship but not their numbers. It is said that only one thing is required to make a group expand: a strong leader. In Mother Ann the Shakers had the essential requisite, but still new members did not join their community. Because the Shakers placed primary importance on the conversion of others, the lack of new members was deeply disheartening. In a world smothered by sin and darkness, they hoped to create a perfect order that would entice the "lost" to join them. How else could they act as pathfinders to God? Yet no new members were added to the little colony. As always, Mother Ann's faith was steadfast. *Testimonies* records her colloquy with her followers during this time of despair:

"O my dear children, hold fast and be not discouraged. God has not sent us to this land in vain, but He has sent us to bring the gospel to this nation which is deeply lost in sin; and there are great numbers who will embrace it, and the time draws nigh."

Elder William Lee then asked Mother, "Do you believe the gospel will ever open to the world?"

Mother replied, "Yea, Brother William, I certainly know it will, and the time is near at hand when they will come like doves."

William replied, "Mother, you have often told us so, but it does not come yet."

Mother said, "Be patient, be patient, O my dear children, for I can see great numbers coming now, and you will soon see them coming in great numbers."

And while they were thus downcast, Mother came out and led them into the forest west of their dwelling where, by the ministrations of the power and gifts of God, through Mother, they had a very joyful meeting, and praised God in songs and dances.

From day to day new converts were expected at Niskeyuna. When they did not appear, the undiscouragable Mother Ann commanded her little family to build up their store of provisions. They obeyed — but still nothing happened. "What is to be done with all this," they asked her, "seeing we are so retired from the world and have so small a company to consume it?"

Mother Ann replied firmly, "We shall have a great company before the close of another year. I see large numbers coming and they will accept and obey the Gospel. I see great men come and bow down their heads and confess their sins. The time draws nigh!"

Another winter gripped the Shakers, more severe than any they had ever known. Biting cold and deep snow compounded their miseries; their dwellings were woefully inadequate for below-zero weather. At last, even Mother Ann sounded dejected. She stood by the icy stream and cried, "O that the fishes of the sea, and the fowls of the air and all things that live and breathe, yea, all the trees of the forest and grass of the fields would pray to God for me."

And *Testimonies* adds poignantly, "Her words were accompanied with tears and heartfelt agony, shared by all who were present."

Chapter Nine

We Do Not Lose Heart

Therefore, having this ministry by the mercy of God, we do not lose heart.

— Second Corinthians,
Chapter 4, verse 1

If true happiness consists of using all of your strength to work for a cause you profoundly believe in, Mother Ann in the wilds of Niskeyuna must have been deeply, satisfyingly happy. Winter and summer she labored without ceasing, exhorting the others to do the same. She wanted everything in readiness when the people "came like doves."

Mother Ann's rule was: love what you do and know that it matters. Her concept of work-as-worship was both a doctrine and a daily discipline. "Be diligent with your hands," she said, "because Godliness does not lead to idleness." But she cautioned her followers not to overwork because that would exalt labor, not God. Only by keeping life simple, she told them, and by cutting away all desire for personal gain, could they reach God.

The Believers followed Mother's example in this, as in all things. They cultivated the land and they culti-vated the spirit — but still no seekers came to Niskeyuna. Some in the small band were discouraged, others actually depressed. Three years had passed since they sailed up the Hudson to open the Shaker mission to the New World. No converts had come and the future looked desolate.

Then, one March day in 1780, something did happen. A great religious revival, led by impassioned Baptists, was convened in New Lebanon, New York, a small town at the foot of the Taconic Mountains. Although the revival took place thirty miles southeast of Niskeyuna, it was to have a strong effect on the Shaker movement.

All sorts of hopeful men and women — rough pioneers and college graduates, poor and well-to-do, old and young — journeyed to New Lebanon seeking spiritual rejuvenation. They were discouraged by the grimness of frontier life, frightened by the havoc of war, guilt-ridden by feelings of sin. All of them wanted the same thing: escape from a hard life. They sought abso-lution of their sins and assurance of a better life in the next world.

Instead of salvation, they discovered at New Lebanon just another battlefield. An angry conflict broke out between the "Old Lights" of the church, who believed people could be saved by faith alone, and the "New Lights" who believed salvation depended on good works. The two groups were locked in combat. Only during worship did the conflicts subside.

The revival services were held, day and night, in a barn belonging to a prosperous farmer named George Darrow. The praying, preaching, and prophesying of the evangelical Baptists culminated in wild singing and shouting. Men and women, transported into religious ecstasies, would fall to the ground "as if wounded in battle." The ecstatic worshippers were convinced the Millennium, the triumphant Second Coming of Christ, was near at hand. Soon their conflicts would be healed, their problems solved. All factions would unite in Christ.

But no Millennium arrived and the fever of religious fervor cooled. Many of the disillusioned revivalists departed. Two who went west, Reuben Wight and Talmadge Bishop, were to become important in the Shaker story. When Wight and Bishop reached Albany, they heard strange tales about a group of "Believers" living in the woods with a female leader scornfully referred to as the "Elect Lady." A female leader? With excited curiosity, the two men took a detour to Niskeyuna.

Mother Ann stood waiting to welcome Reuben Wight and Talmadge Bishop. She said she had been expecting them — a premonition told her they were approaching. She invited the two men to spend the night and join the Shakers in worship, which they did.

The visitors were amazed by everything they saw and heard. Is it possible, they asked, that the Christ we have waited for in vain actually has come, as these devout people claim — and in the form of a *woman*?

The Shakers' answer was a resounding yes.

"It is true," said Mother Ann. "I am the embodiment of the Christ spirit. But you, too, can experience that in-dwelling presence, if you will forsake the world and the flesh and let yourself be imbued by his consuming love."

She told them salvation is not an event. There would never be a universal day of judgment for all mankind. Salvation, said Mother Ann, is a quiet transformation that takes place within an individual who enters wholly into the life of the spirit. For a person who has been "saved," the world and all its desires melt away and the Millennium begins.

When the visitors protested that such ideas amounted to revolution, she replied calmly, "We are the people who turn the world upside down."

Fired by Mother Ann's spiritual intensity, Wight and Bishop hastened back to New Lebanon to tell the others about this extraordinary female. They described her as having the physical courage and spiritual strength of a male. The only way they could relate to such a powerful woman was to compare her to a man.

In truth, Mother Ann was far more feminine than she was masculine. *A Summary View* states: "By many of the world who saw her without prejudice she was called beautiful; and to her faithful children she appeared to possess a degree of dignified beauty and heavenly love which they had never before discovered among mortals."

Two leaders of the New Lebanon revival, the Reverend Joseph Meacham and the Reverend Samuel Johnson, listened attentively to the glowing descriptions of the Shakers and their female "lead." They decided to send one of their strongest associates, Calvin Harlow, to Niskeyuna to interrogate this singular woman.

Harlow was given the exact question to put to the woman in the woods who claimed to be invested with the authority of Christ. The encounter between

Calvin Harlow and Mother Ann was a turning point. Their exchange was preserved in Shaker history:

> Calvin Harlow: "Saint Paul said:*'Let your women keep silence in the Churches; for it is not permitted unto them to speak; but they are commanded to be under obedience, as also saith the law. And if they will learn any thing, let them ask their husbands at home; for it is a shame for a woman to speak in the Church.'* But you, Lady, you not only speak, you seem to be an Elder in your Church. How do you reconcile that with the doctrine of the Apostle Paul?"
>
> Mother Ann: "The order of nature requires a man and a woman to produce offspring. . . . He is the Father and she is the Mother; and all the children, both male and female, must be subject to their parents . . . but when the man is gone, the right of government belongs to the woman. So it is with the family of Christ."

Apparently, Calvin Harlow was completely won over. Whether it was Mother Ann's powerful personality or her strong logic — or both — we do not know. We do know that he hurried back to New Lebanon and reported to the Reverend Meacham that the long-awaited Second Coming had indeed occurred — and in the body of a woman.

Of course, Joseph Meacham was dubious. He set out at once for Niskeyuna to examine for himself this electrifying "woman of the new birth," and he took two other Baptists with him. Meacham was a solid citizen, not given to fantasy. A forty-year-old Baptist minister from Enfield, Connecticut, he was a well-known religious leader. His opinion would carry weight.

Meacham's confrontation with Mother Ann must have been dramatic. They met in the woods near Niskeyuna on a morning in May. The stern American Baptist and his two brethren stood on one side. Mother Ann, small and dynamic, stood opposite them, her chief disciple James Whittaker at her side.

According to *Testimonies*, Brother Meacham said, "If you have attained to that of God which we have not, we should be glad to share with you; for we want to find the best way to be saved."

For some reason, Mother Ann designated James Whittaker as her spokesman. Perhaps she thought, as most people did, that men listen best to men. "If you are to be saved by Christ," he said, "you must walk as he walked. And if you have committed sins, you must confess them to witnesses in whom Christ has taken up his abode."

"Are you perfect?" challenged the Baptist Meacham. "Do you live without sin?"

Whittaker's answer was firm. "The Power of God does indeed enable souls to cease from sin; and we have received that power. We have actually left off committing sin, and we live in daily obedience to the will of God."

Mother Ann could no longer keep silent. "Sin is gratification of self!" she cried. "Only through celibacy can true Godliness be achieved. You must forsake the marriage of flesh, or you cannot be married to the Lamb."

Their dialogue continued all day, interrupted only for worship. By evening, the Reverend Meacham and his companions had fallen under Mother Ann's spell. She offered them a program more exciting and more specific than anything they had found at the

revival, or within their own faith. The Shaker require-
ments, Mother told them, were precise. They must separate themselves from the material world, shun all sex,
and confess all sins. Then, perhaps, by living in monas-
tic simplicity and sharing all their worldly wealth with
their sisters and brothers, they would be able to reach
God in work and in worship. The cost was high — total
denial of self; but the promised reward was great:
"at-oneness" with God.

She must have been compelling. The Reverend
Joseph Meacham, chief Baptist pastor in the district of
New Lebanon, became Mother Ann's first important
convert in America. She called him her "first-born son"
and predicted that when she died, Joseph Meacham
would hold the Believers together.

Meacham's wife and children, his father and
other relatives also joined the Believers. The addition of
children to the colony was vital since the society's pro-
hibition against sexual intercourse obviously meant
there would be no children to carry the United Society
of Believers into the next generation.

News of the Reverend Mr. Meacham's conver-
sion spread rapidly. Soon other seekers journeyed to
Niskeyuna. Inspired by Mother Ann's eloquence, many
of them became Shakers. Some were simple folk like
Talmadge Bishop, others important people like George
Darrow and the Reverend Samuel Johnson.

Johnson, who graduated from Yale in 1769, was
followed into the Shaker faith by his wife, Elizabeth.
The reasons they gave for joining are interesting.
Samuel Johnson said, "While at Niskeyuna I witnessed
divine power. Listening to Mother Ann, my own conscience was salved and I received a true baptism of the
Holy Spirit."

His wife's explanation is more down-to-earth. Elizabeth Johnson had married a minister of the Gospel when she was twenty-four hoping, she said, to be living nearer to God, "for the spirit of worship is strong within me." Instead, she found disappointment in a marriage which seemed to keep her from God, and that was why she became "greatly interested in the self-denying way of these people called Shakers."

Other married couples joined the Shakers, some bringing their children to be loved and cared for by the community. Why would husbands and wives want to belong to a sect that forbade sexual intercourse? Did they agree with Mother Ann's statement, "The root of all human depravity is the sexual relationship originating with Adam and Eve?" Were they trying to avoid parenthood? Were some women seeking the equality with men which Shakers, unlike the society around them, were able to accept? The questions are endless; the answers unclear.

But for the United Society of Believers nothing was unclear. They stated as a fundamental principle: "The object of Shaker life is self-conquest . . . it is to die to the corrupt, passionate animal life of the world that we may be resurrected in pure and angelic societies."

Chapter Ten

Celibacy and Separation of the Sexes

Near Albany they settled
And waited for a while,
Until a mighty shaking
Made all the desert smile.
At length a gentle whisper,
The tidings did convey
And many flocked to Mother
To learn the living way.

— Early Shaker Spiritual

The Shaker community in the wilderness began to expand after the New Lebanon revival. Mother Ann, watching her little colony grow, quoted the prophecy of Isaiah: *The wilderness and the solitary place shall be glad for them; and the desert shall rejoice and blossom as the rose.*

People were attracted to Niskeyuna by the rumors about Mother Ann. It was said her faith was so intense that anyone who got near her could absorb it. Her rapid conversion of the two prominent Baptist ministers, the Reverend Joseph Meacham and the Reverend Samuel Johnson, spread her fame, but it aroused antagonism as well.

Some feared that this strange woman threatened the very fabric of society. Everything she stood for was dangerous: the rejection of clergy, creeds, liturgies, and sacraments; the refusal to take oaths or bear arms; the dedication to communal living and common ownership of property; the insistence on the "obvious" (to her) fact that preaching, teaching, and prophecy were as appropriate for women as for men — scandalous suggestions, all.

Most shocking was Mother Ann's open hostility toward marriage. When she announced that marriage was a stumbling block on the path to spiritual fulfillment, she seemed to strike at civilization itself. Mother claimed biblical authority and quoted Saint Paul, 1 Corinthians 7:32–33, to prove it. *"He that is unmarried careth for the things that belong to the Lord, how he may please the Lord: But he that is married careth for things that are of the world, how he may please his wife."*

To eighteenth-century Americans struggling to establish order on a crude frontier, her ideas smacked of witchcraft. Any woman who was against the institution of marriage must be some kind of a devil. Mother Ann made a puzzling reply to this charge: "The devil is a real being, as real as a bear. I know, for I have seen him and fought with him."

The Believers concurred when Mother Ann told them "weakness of the flesh" was the cause of all sinfulness — vanity, greed, vulgarity, sloth, extravagance, disorder, dishonesty. They said her attackers were the problem, not she. As Aurelia Mace explained in *The Aletheia*: "Mother called people away from selfish family life into a great brotherhood and sisterhood, and struck a deadly blow against those indulgences which the carnally minded so much desired."

Mother Ann did nothing to mollify her critics. *Testimonies* describes one occasion when she came into a room where there were a number of married couples and announced, "I see a vision, a large black cloud rising as black as a thunder cloud, and it is occasioned by men sleeping with their wives." Mother admonished them not do it any more.

On another occasion, she said to a woman with five children, "Are you not ashamed to live in the filthy works of the flesh? You must go and take up your cross and put your hands to work and your heart to God." *Take up your cross* was a phrase the Shakers often used to refer to their renunciation of sex. Such statements threatened to ignite the overheated atmosphere that surrounded "the prophetess".

The Shaker way was not for everyone. Mother Ann understood that. She had an uncanny ability to put herself in another's place. To those who found celibacy impossible, she again quoted Saint Paul: *If they cannot contain, let them marry: for it is better to marry than to burn.*

According to *Testimonies*, a convert who had been married to the handsome, strong-minded Shakeress Lucy Wright, came to Mother Ann and said it was out of the question for him to suppress his sexual desires. She answered him with great kindness: "I was once as you are. I had feet but they walked in forbidden paths. I had hands and they handled unclean things. I had eyes but they saw nothing of God aright. But now my eyes see, my ears hear, and my hands handle the Word of Life."

Improving the status of women was of paramount importance to Mother Ann. She clearly perceived the long and painful battle they would have to fight to gain freedom of mind and body. She was determined to help free them from oppression. For generations, the supremacy of man had been accepted as biblical truth inspired by God. Mother Ann was one of the few spiritual leaders to repudiate the time-honored hoax of women's inferiority which began with Adam and Eve. Even so strong a religious reformer as Martin Luther could sneer, "Women were created with large hips so they can stay home and sit on them."

Starting with the founder's powerful example, equality of the sexes permeated Shaker life. Women conducted worship or spoke at meetings and they were as influential as men. Undergirding these revolutionary departures was Mother Ann's belief, so central to Shaker religion, in the duality of God. God was the "Eternal Two" who encompassed both fatherhood and motherhood.

"In the Shaker Community," Shakeress Aurelia Mace wrote in 1907, "woman has taken her place as an equal with man, by intellectual if not by physical strength. Where there is an Elder, there is also an Elderess; where there is a Deacon, there is also a Deaconess, and they are considered equal in their powers of government." Incredibly, the Shakers achieved this kind of equality at a time when no woman could have found employment equal to that of a man. Small wonder people were angered by the audacity of Mother Ann.

Because she understood that temptation was a constant threat to celibacy, Mother devised modes of "lodging together." She wanted to build a new kind of relationship between men and women that rested on the twin pillars of equality of the sexes and separation of the sexes. For the Shakers, separation was essential. The brethren and the sisters were never permitted to be together alone and all living arrangements were completely separate. At meetings women entered through

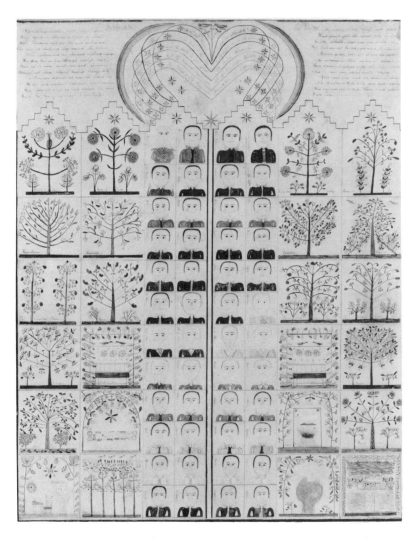

A sample of a spirit drawing, which Shakers rendered as agents of the spirit. In this Emblem of the Heavenly Sphere, attributed to Sister Polly Collins of Hancock, Massachusetts, the artist depicted her notion of Heaven, which includes forty-eight smiling saintachusetts and early Shaker leaders. Mother Ann, her brother William, and her faithful follower James Whittaker appear at the top along with Christopher Columbus, whose discovery of the New World, chosen home of the Shakers, may explain his honored position. Below Mother Ann, the Savior raises his hands in benediction. Courtesy of Hancock Shaker Village, Pittsfield, Massachusetts.

one door, men through another; the women sat on one side of the room, the men on the other. Touching of any kind was forbidden, even shaking hands.

Mother Ann felt that if men and women did not have some kind of informal relationship "they would surely have a carnal one"; therefore, she originated "union meetings." Three times a week the brothers and sisters met together, sitting face-to-face, and spent one hour "in friendly social intercourse with each other." They talked or read or sang.

Dancing, also part of "lodging together," was useful in helping to sublimate sexual urges. Many people think of dancing as exciting sexual desire, but for the Shakers the opposite was true. During that rhythmic part of their worship, they gave vent to their inner turmoil. As Shakerism developed, dancing became less abandoned and more precise, but even then it was considered a valuable safety valve that could release the faithful from terrorizing anxieties.

One observer described the Shakers "swiftly passing and repassing each other like clouds agitated by a mighty wind." Moving in square or circular formations they sang, clapped, and stamped, bowing and bending, often shaking out their hands before them, as if to get rid of evil and sin through the fingertips. Or dancing with palms upturned, to symbolize the receiving of blessings. Their dancing is depicted in this "gift song". For the Shakers, singing was as important as breathing.

Who will bow and bend like a willow,
Who will turn and twist and reel
In the gale of simple freedom,
From the bower of union flowing?

Who will drink the wine of power,
Dropping down like a shower?
Pride and bondage all forgetting,
Mother's wine is freely working.

Oh ho! I will have it,
I will bow and bend to get it,
I'll be reeling, turning, twisting,
Shake out all the starch and stiff'ning!

When the Shaker dancing grew ecstatic, wild whirling caused some dancers to faint. Pious neighbors declared combining worship with dance was blasphemy. Mother Ann was ready, as always, with an answer : "We take our authority from the Bible," she said, reminding them that after he slew Goliath, David "danced with all his might before the Ark of the Lord."

Mother Ann reinforced the requirement of celibacy with constant preaching and exhorting. "If you fight against the lust of the flesh," she said, "you offer to God the first fruits of your lives. There is a glorious crown for all who struggle against the flesh in this world."

In the place of sex, she urged tenderness, compassion, caring. She said Jesus called each person to be father, mother, brother, sister to everyone he or she encountered. She asked for the abandonment of sexual roles, and even age roles. "We are not called to be one thing or the other — male or female, old or young," she said. "We are called to show forth the Divine — to be all things to all people."

After Mother Ann's death, Shaker regulations for separation of the sexes became picayune, with ridiculous prohibitions such as: *Brethren and sisters may not pass each other on the stairs. Whispering is not permitted and blinking should never be practiced.* They even included this odd injunction: *Sisters must not mend, nor set buttons, on brethren's clothes, while they have them on.*

The rejection of sex by the Shakers has always excited curiosity. Many people, repelled by the whole idea, ridiculed their chastity vows. Unrealistic, unhealthy, unchristian, impossible, they said. But the remarkable thing is that no significant case of sexual scandal ever erupted in a Shaker community. Those who were angered by the peculiarities of Shaker life did not get close enough to discover that these people were trying to create a Utopian society, ruled by the gentle law of love, where every hand was lifted for work and every heart bowed to God.

Since all Believers followed the strict rule of celibacy, how could the Society possibly maintain membership? The answer is, new members were obtained by conversion, by recruiting, and — in the case of children — by adoption. At a time when there were no institutions to take care of orphaned, abandoned, or illegitimate children, the Shakers lovingly welcomed them. These children did not become Shakers automatically. They had to make the decision for themselves after they came of age.

Mother Ann bore her neighbors' hostility philosophically. She knew it would be a long time before the United Society of Believers was accepted. But she was not one to wait around for miracles; her way was to make miracles happen. The time had come, she decided, to send a missionary out into the world to tell the story of the Shaker faith and look for converts. She selected a dashing spokesman — her brother William Lee.

A tall, handsome man with long curly hair, Brother William must have had the magnetic Lee personality. Like their father, he started out as a blacksmith in Manchester. Then he abandoned the family craft for a more glamorous career — he joined a royal cavalry regiment, the Oxford Blues. *Testimonies* describes the youthful William a bit critically, as "a proud haughty young man, fond of gayety and able to dress himself in silks."

Before long, William Lee wearied of high living and "fell into great trouble of mind because of his sins." Sickened by his own excesses, he decided to consult his sister Ann, then a pious young member of Manchester's Wardley Society. *Testimonies* continues the story: "When he arrived at his sister's being very gaily dressed, she reproved him for his pride, and convinced him of the wickedness of his life. He threw off his ruffles and silks and labored faithfully to find forgiveness for his sins and acceptance of God." At his sister's instigation, he made a detailed confession of his sins.

Mother Ann was ahead of her time in her understanding of guilt. She refused to accept the prevailing view that the proper treatment for guilty feelings was repetitive prayer, followed by self-inflicted punishment. She knew from experience that the power generated by guilt could provide energy for change. She *knew* guilt could blossom into renewal of spirit.

Her basic solution for the ubiquitous problem of guilt was simple: confession. After a repeated outpouring of sins, the sinner was to seek atonement in work and worship. Brother William followed her instructions faithfully — and his whole way of life changed.

The conversion of her brother from playboy to penitent is one more evidence of Mother Ann's power. Though she was only four years older, William depended on her guidance. She so awakened his conscience that he felt his soul was "upon a needle's point."

Renouncing his profession, home, family, and friends, he joined the Shakers.

Just as with the others, Mother Ann became William's guiding star. He said, "I love my Mother — although she is my Sister, yet she has become my Mother, and the Lord God has made me to love her."

In America, Brother William Lee — "a man of sorrows, acquainted with grief" — was to become the first itinerant Shaker minister, and a good one. Blessed with natural charm, he was a fine singer, a skillful horseman, and an eloquent speaker. It was said he could do anything from laying out a garden in perfect order to drowning an accuser in a torrent of "bold language."

Brother William apparently shared his sister's flaming talent for transmitting his feelings and his convictions to others, for he brought numerous men and women into the Shaker faith. One of his early converts was a woman with the apt name of Thankful Barce. In *Testimonies* Thankful records what it was like to join the United Society of Believers:

> When I arrived, Mother Ann met me at the door, took hold of my hand and led me into the house. Her first salutation to me was in these words: "Being a daughter of Zion, how camest thou hither without a cap on thy head?"
>
> She sat down in a chair, and I sat down by her side. Her eyes were shut, and it appeared that her sense was withdrawn from the things of time. She sung very melodiously, and appeared very beautiful. . . . The graceful motion of her hands, the beautiful appearance of her countenance, and the heavenly melody of her voice, made her seem like

a glorious inhabitant of the heavenly world,
singing praises to God.

   As I sat by the side of her, one of her hands,
while in motion, frequently touched my arm; and
at every touch of her hand, I instantly felt the
power of God run through my whole body.

   Clearly, Mother Ann had charisma. The Greek
word for "divine gift," *charisma* originally was used to
describe the miraculous powers that early Christians
were said to possess — powers to heal, speak in
tongues, and prophesy. Mother Ann's disciples also
claimed miraculous gifts of grace for her, but she was
careful never to presume godlike powers for herself. To
those who came seeking forgiveness of their sins,
Testimonies says Mother Ann would declare: "I pray
God to forgive you. It is God that forgives you. I am but
your fellow servant."

Chapter Eleven

Mother Ann, Spy

Behold it is a time of war
And we have been enlisting,
Emmanuel we're fighting for,
And Satan we're resisting;
We have not in this war begun
To turn our backs as traitors,
But we will all unite as one
Against our carnal natures.

— Early Shaker Spiritual

On May 10, 1780 — New England's famous "Dark Day" — the sun never came out. Fearful souls, wringing their hands and wailing in the darkness, cried, "The day of Judgment has come!" It happened that was the day Mother Ann had selected for the first public testimony at Niskeyuna. No wonder people thought the woman possessed supernatural power. A Baptist minister named Issachar Bates describes that epic day in his autobiography.

> There were neither clouds nor smoke in the atmosphere, yet the sun did not appear. . . . No work could be done in any houses without a candle! . . . The darkness covered the whole of the land of New England! And what next, right on the back

of this came on the Shakers! And that made it darker yet . . . it was singing, dancing, shouting, shaking, speaking with tongues, turning, preaching, prophesying, and warning the world to confess their sins and turn to God. . . .

All this was right in the neighborhood where I lived.

The Shakers' behavior during the Dark Day crisis made a deep impression, Issachar Bates wrote. They turned to God while others reacted by "cursing, blaspheming . . . and firing pistols." Tempted to join the new movement, he added somewhat wistfully, "But I was not ready yet, for I had married a wife." Later Elder Bates did bring his wife and seven children into the faith and helped to carry Shakerism into Kentucky and Ohio.

The first Testimony attracted people. Under the dynamic leadership of Mother Ann and Brother William, Shaker membership began to increase. But their enemies were also increasing. According to *A Summary View,* "Such a remarkable event [the conversion of large numbers to Shakerism] could not take place without exciting great agitation in the public mind. Hence many conjectures were in circulation concerning these strange people, and especially concerning their female leader. By some she was strongly suspected of witchcraft, and the old accusation was in substance revived: 'She casteth out devils by Beelzebub.' "

At this time, the American Revolution was spreading into the upper part of New York, and zealous patriots began to fan the fires of suspicion that already smoldered around the British-born folk at Niskeyuna. After the Yankees trounced the Red Coats at Saratoga, it was widely feared that the English navy would retaliate by sailing up the Hudson and cutting the colonies in two. Albany, a strategic point of utmost importance, was gripped by hysteria and anyone in the area who had Loyalist leanings was considered dangerous.

Suddenly rumors about the Shakers proliferated. It was said Niskeyuna was the hiding place for a network of British spies, directed by a sinister woman who called herself "the Female Christ." Soon the Shakers were threatened with the kind of persecution they thought they had left behind in England.

The noted historian Henry Steele Commager says the most important item in the American Constitution is freedom of religion. This precious guarantee did not come easily. The struggle for religious freedom in America is a long and bitter story. Those who made the dangerous journey to this country seeking "freedom of worship" were not always willing to confer that right on others. Men and women who held unorthodox beliefs were hounded and abused in the New World as they had been in the old.

Anne Hutchinson, for example, was tried and ordered to leave the Massachusetts Bay Colony for preaching that true religion was found, not in a church, but by following an "inner light." Roger Williams was tried and banished from Massachusetts for his insistence on the separation of church and state. Mary Dyer, a devout Quaker, was repeatedly arrested in Boston on the strange charge of "bearing witness to her faith." She was accused of sedition, condemned to death, and hanged in Boston Common.

Mother Ann is a less well-known but equally staunch figure in the procession of early Americans who bravely endured persecution for the sake of their religious convictions. From the very beginning, she decreed that Shakers, like their Quaker colleagues, must be pacifists. As followers in Christ's footsteps, they were never to aid or abet the sins of war and bloodshed. Mother Ann forbade her followers, absolutely, to fight anyone for any cause whatsoever.

"Arm yourselves only with meekness and patience," she told her followers. The Believers, dedicated to the salvation of their souls, understood her; but outsiders thought only a British spy would suggest such a thing. The burghers of Albany, preparing to fight the enemy on home ground, had no sympathy for the Shakers' so-called "conscientious objection." Crying "Tories!", they demanded that all Shakers swear loyalty to America. *Testimonies* gives us Mother Ann's reaction to that idea:

> General James Sullivan, with two other men of note, came to require the Elders to take the oath of allegiance to the country. The Elders refused to take the oath, and Mother Ann said to the General, "These men will never do you any hurt for they are well-wishers to the country. They will do all the good to the country that they are able to do."
>
> The General replied, "I want men to go and fight for the country."
>
> Mother answered, "You will never kill the devil with the sword."

It was impossible for the patriots to understand that the Believers at Niskeyuna simply had no interest whatever in patriotism or in politics. To the Shakers, America was just one small part of God's earth. It was the favored ground on which the kingdom of the Lord was first to be established, and they said of course they would cherish it. Fight for it they would not.

The more the Shakers tried to explain their position, the more they were considered suspect. When they began transporting extra food to Niskeyuna to feed their new converts, the patriots decided that they were supplying the British army with food and ammunition, while spying on the side. The festering boil of suspicion came to a head on a July day in 1780. David Darrow and Joseph Meacham were driving a flock of sheep along the road toward Niskeyuna when they were attacked by an angry mob. The two Shakers were captured and thrown into the Albany jail. The sheep were divided up among the crowd.

Mother Ann, Brother William, and James Whittaker were also arrested and thrown into the prison. All were accused of disloyalty to the American cause. But the real objective may have been to get rid of these queer people who were enticing solid citizens into deserting home, church, and country.

Again the authorities demanded that the Shakers take an oath of allegiance. Again Mother Ann refused. She repeated that her people would have nothing to do with the Revolutionary War. Some years later, Mother Ann's pacifist convictions were codified in the Shakers' "Peace Document":

> Were mankind divested of pride and ambition, all wars would cease. . . . We believe God has called us to this very work; and that it is required of us to set the example of peace and to maintain it at all hazards. . . . We are firmly persuaded that those who subject themselves to the cross of Christ, and

after his example, subdue the evil propensities
which lead to war and strife, render more essential
service to their country than they possibly could by
bearing arms and aiding war.

The Shaker arguments fell on deaf ears. Their
leaders were charged with maintaining a secret correspondence with the enemy and publicly accused of
treason.

Treason! What a dire word for peace-loving gen-
tlefolk to deal with! Back in England there had been two
kinds of treason: high treason — the killing of a head of
state; and petty treason — the killing of a husband by a
wife or a master by a servant. (If the wife were killed by
the husband, that was a much less serious crime.) High
treason was punished by public hanging, followed by
drawing and quartering of the traitor's body.

In colonial America, distinctions were not so
clear-cut. Treason was defined as attempting to over-
throw the government to which one owed allegiance.
But which government was that? Many clergymen, for
instance, still believed in the divine right of kings and,
as members of the Anglican church, said daily prayers
for King George III and his family. These ministers were
not accused of treason — but then they were not, like
the Shakers, asking people to reject the accepted values
of society.

The jail in the Old Fort at Albany was cold and
forbidding. Mother Ann, having spent so much time in
prison in England, must have felt right at home. She
knew how to outwit confinement with her eloquent
tongue and she attracted large crowds by preaching
through the grates of her prison window.

She told the people who gathered to hear her

that faith in God would carry them through any crisis. Thinking perhaps of her miraculous escape from death aboard the storm-tossed *Mariah*, she added, "Faith is the anchor of the soul. It is like an anchor to a ship when the winds blow and the waves run high. So, in like manner, faith will keep the soul steady in trials, temptations, and buffetings."

"Buffetings" is exactly what Mother Ann had to face. To silence her, the Americans decided they would ship the preaching woman back to the British who held New York City. Let the Tories cope with this female who conversed with God in an English accent. Waging a revolution was difficult enough without having some woman, who drew people like a magnet and kept repeating, over and over: "No one who lives by wars and bloodshed can follow Christ."

The authorities placed the "Elect Lady," as they jeeringly called her, on a sloop headed for Manhattan Island. They hoped that was the last they would hear of her. Shakeress Mary Partington, at her own request, was allowed to accompany her.

Mother Ann's boat got only as far as Poughkeepsie. Again she was put in jail. *Testimonies* says:

> During Mother Ann's confinement in Poughkeepsie jail, she was generally treated with kindness; and Mary, who was not considered as a prisoner, had full liberty to procure necessaries for her at the groceries. But for most of the time, she was under great sufferings of soul; being deeply impressed with the importance of the work before her, and feeling that her infant spiritual children had great need of her presence and protection, her soul was in continual cries to God.

Mary Hocknell made the journey from the Niskeyuna settlement to Poughkeepsie to try to rescue Mother. She lodged with one James Boyd and his wife Nancy and, predictably, the Boyds soon confessed their sins and "embraced the Testimony." James Boyd must have been a man of influence because he managed to get Mother Ann removed from jail and confined to his house instead.

At the Boyds', Mother Ann, her two female companions, and their hosts "often engaged in the worship of God, under the great power and operations of the spirit." *Testimonies* describes the local reaction to their strange services. The picture of the citizens of Poughkeepsie trying to burn out people at prayer is not pretty.

> Their behavior began to excite opposition among some of the lower class of people in the town of Poughkeepsie. . . . One night, in particular, a number of the baser sort, painted and habited after the manner of Indians, came and surrounded the house, while the people were in the worship of God, and attempted to throw papers of gunpowder, through the windows into the fire, but, failing in their attempt, and being discovered, and sharply reproved by Mother Ann and James Boyd, they withdrew.
>
> The attempt was secretly renewed some time in the night, and a large paper of powder thrown in at the top of the chimney, but fortunately, it bounded from the hearth, and did not take fire.

Following this crisis, Mother Ann was taken back to the Poughkeepsie jail. Meanwhile, the Elders were suffering similar indignities in the Albany prison. One of them, the Reverend Samuel Johnson, was declared insane because his brother pleaded for Samuel's release on the grounds that he was out of his mind, "being *formerly* devoted to the cause of his country and zealous to defend her liberties by force of arms."

The Reverend Mr. Johnson was discharged after his brother promised to make sure that he left the state, and David Darrow was paroled after his well-to-do father-in-law, Captain Jarvis Mudge, interceded. Eventually, the others were released without a trial. All except Mother Ann. Apparently the authorities were afraid to let the leader go.

Oddly enough, imprisonment worked in favor of the Shakers. Some patriots rallied to help them, saying their treatment smacked of the kind of tyranny people had come to this country to escape. Even in the midst of Revolution, there were those who dared to speak out for civil liberty when they saw defenseless people denied it.

The Shakers' prime objective was to free Mother Ann. The whole future of the United Society of Believers depended on the liberation of their leader. She had been jailed in August, and it was now winter. Her followers ferried across the icy Hudson, hired a horse and carriage, and drove seventy miles over slippery roads to Poughkeepsie to demand her release. To their dismay, the local constabulary flatly refused to discharge "the grand actress," as they called her. They claimed she was a dangerous spy in the pay of the British.

The Elders did everything they could to free her, but with no success. There was, finally, one thing left to try: an appeal to the governor. It was decided Elder James Whittaker should seek help from Governor George Clinton. Known as "The Father of New York State," Clinton enjoyed great popularity. He was elected Governor of New York seven times and Vice President of the United States twice, first with Thomas Jefferson, then with James Madison.

At the time Elder James called on him in Poughkeepsie, Clinton was forty-one and had been governor only three years. He was a handsome, somewhat plump, man-of-the-people whose election had been a jolt to the establishment. The patrician John Jay wrote, "Clinton's family and connections do not entitle him to so distinguished a pre-eminence."

George Clinton was known for "frankness and amiability in private life," but he must have seemed formidable to Elder James Whittaker. The governor was an intensely patriotic military man, said to be unmerciful to Tories. The gentle, devout Shaker approached him with trepidation. *Testimonies* says of their encounter:

> Elder James informed the Governor of their
> imprisonment, and related the pretense of accusa-
> tion, and the manner of their treatment and suffer-
> ings. The Governor said it was the first knowledge
> he had received of the matter; and that he did not
> know there was such a woman in prison. Elder
> James, on his knees, besought the Governor's
> assistance.

The sight of Elder James kneeling before him apparently moved George Clinton. He said he certainly was not in sympathy with jailing people for their religious beliefs. "In view of the length of incarceration," the Governor declared, "and due to lack of any treasonable evidence, aside from her refusal of oath, I believe the woman should be freed."

James Whittaker was required to post a two-hundred-pound bond for Mother Ann's "good behavior." This he was able to do with help from Brother William Lee. They promised that she would not "say or consent to any Matters or Things inconsistent with the Peace and safety of this the United States" — and then Mother Ann was released.

With great rejoicing, the Brethren took Mother and her companions, Mary Partington and Mary Hocknell, back to Niskeyuna. At the end of December 1780, *Testimonies* says Mother Ann "was joyfully received by all her faithful children, 'in spiritual relation,' after an absence of nearly five months. Thus ended the only imprisonment that ever Mother Ann suffered in America. . . . By means of this event . . . the fame of 'Christ's Second Appearing' extended far and wide." The happy Believers made up songs in praise of conscience:

> *Rights of conscience in these days,*
> *Now demand our solemn praise;*
> *Here we see what God has done,*
> *By his servant Washington,*
> *Who with wisdom was endow'd*
> *By an angel, through the cloud,*
> *And led forth, in wisdom's plan,*
> *To secure the rights of man.*

It is interesting to note that twenty years later, long after the death of Mother Ann, Governor Clinton paid a visit to the Shakers in New Lebanon and expressed his pride in having "released their spiritual Mother from durance vile."

The Shakers and the Quakers were the first organized groups in America to speak out for conscientious objection to all wars. For Mother Ann, ultimate loyalty belonged not to a man-made law but to a peace-loving God. On this firm conviction she took her stand like Milton's faithful seraph Abdiel, "unmoved, unshaken, unseduced, unterrified."

Mother Ann Lee may have been more important to the new nation than many of her more famous contemporaries. For, in the words of Henry Steele Commager, "Those willing to sacrifice for conscience are the most valuable members of any society."

Chapter Twelve

Enemies

No one ever saved anybody, or served
any great cause, or left any enduring
impress, who was not willing to forget
indignities, bear no grudges. The
world's saviors have all, in one way or
another, loved their enemies and done
them good.

— The Reverend Harry Emerson Fosdick

Mother Ann could be called the avatar of the Shaker movement. To the Hindus, who originated the word, an avatar was a God who appeared on earth in bodily form. Although Mother Ann was not a God to the Shakers, she was indeed the embodiment of all their religious beliefs.

The safe return of their avatar, after five months in the foul prisons of Albany and Poughkeepsie, brought unbridled rejoicing to Niskeyuna. Singing, dancing, and praying resounded far into the night. Many were angry over Mother Ann's mistreatment, but she reproved them. "You can never enter into the Kingdom of God with hardness against anyone," she said. "God is love, and if you love God you will love one another."

Perhaps it was Mother Ann's obsession with the Kingdom of God, the "completely other," that most attracted people. For pious folk who felt a vacuum within, her intensity must have been hypnotic. They expected her to lift the whirling mists of daily life and show them the shining world of the spirit.

Not surprisingly, a number of people who eagerly joined the Shaker crusade were sorely disappointed. Their attempts at an entirely new life were blocked by timidity, skepticism, shame, isolation, and fear. Exposure to religious ecstasy, instead of freeing them from the iron grip of anxiety, increased their tensions. Mother Ann's all-consuming passion for perfection demanded too much. To reject everything worldly, even sexual intercourse, was beyond most people. And confession of the sins that lay buried deep within was impossible. Some who were disillusioned and disappointed became her enemies.

No matter what accusations were hurled at Mother Ann, she turned the other cheek. "Keep a strict watch over the words you speak," she told her followers, "that you may not treat others unkindly, nor cast on them unpleasant reflections. Let your words be few and seasoned with grace."

The Believers, who called the induction into Shakerism "a time of sifting", were philosophical about those who "proved unworthy." They divided the ones who were left into three groups: Winter Shakers, Bread-and-Butter Shakers, and Mortal Enemies.

Winter Shakers enjoyed the comfort and warmth of the community during the cold months, but when the robins sang, they departed. Mother Ann is quoted in *Testimonies* as telling them, "It is now spring of the year, and you have all had the privilege of being taught the way of God. Now you may all go home and be faithful with your hands. Every faithful man will go forth and put up his fences in season, and will plow his ground in season; and such a man may with confidence look for a blessing." A few of the faithful tried to follow her instructions. The others slipped back into old routines and let the discipline of Niskeyuna fade away.

Bread-and-Butter Shakers were nourished briefly by Mother Ann's spiritual diet, but could not muster enough self-discipline to meet the stringent daily demands. A laconic notation in an early Shaker record book says: "John Short, Henry and George Grubb ran off to the world." The same book shows how the Believers dealt with those converts who were unable to give up the "fats and creams" of everyday life: "Lucy Lemons was kindly invited to go to the world. She went."

Mortal Enemies were the most difficult to cope with. They were the men and women who, for various reasons, left the society — and then launched vitriolic attacks against the Shakers. One of the most vituperative was a Baptist minister from Stonington, Connecticut, named Valentine Rathbun. Refusal by The Shakers to bear arms in the Revolution, or even take an oath of allegiance, infuriated Brother Valentine. He departed in a rage, accusing them of being un-American, pro-British, pro-Catholic (celibacy and confession being identified with Roman Catholicism), pagan, and immoral.

The Reverend Mr. Rathbun proceeded to write a pamphlet called "Some Brief Hints of a Religious Scheme Taught and Propagated by a Number of Europeans Living in a Place Called Nisquenia, [*sic*] in the State of New York." It was published in 1785. Since his booklet contains the earliest eyewitness account of a Shaker meeting, it is worth examination, bearing in mind that Valentine Rathbun's anti-Shaker, anti-British prejudice bordered on fanaticism. He reinforces his violent indignation with exclamation points.

> To obtain instruction from the woman preacher, Ann Lee, I went to "Nisquenia" and gave her a lengthy relation of my life. In return, she made me many wonderful promises. . . .
>
> Shakerism is a religion of bluff and its adherents are fanatics. . . . I myself beheld the following, and know, therefore, whereof I speak. . . .
>
> They meet together in the dead of night and have been heard two miles by people. . . . They run about in the woods and elsewhere, hooting and tooting like owls. . . .
>
> Very extraordinary but wicked movements in worship cause the Believers to gape, stretch, and twitch as though in convulsions. As these fits increase, so does faith in the Shaker leader, Ann Lee.
>
> If onlookers try to bring worshippers out of these curious shakings and quiverings, other worshippers cry out that the onlookers will be damned for opposing the will of God. Meanwhile, the victims are twitching and trembling as though afflicted by a terrible ague. Following this violence, sudden acute weakness sets in and the worshippers fall helplessly to the floor. . . .
>
> Some Shakers sing songs. Some sing without words in Indian dialects. Others sing jigs or tunes of their own making which they call "new tongues."

While some dance, others jump up and down — all this going on at the same time until the different tunes, groaning, jumping, dancing, the drumming, laughing, talking, fluttering, shoving, and hissing, make such a bedlam as only the insane can thrive upon.

This Ann Lee calls the worship of God! She speaks highly of her elders, too, and says those men of hers are the Angels of God sent to gather God's Elect! As for herself, she has this to say: "I have the fullness of the Godhead bodily dwelling in me. . . . Yea, Christ, through me, is born the second time!"

Anybody opposing this blasphemy is threatened with eternal damnation!

Most of those who join Ann Lee's movement are urged to cry out against the military defense of the country, against fighting the common British foe! All authority, I have heard her say — is from Hell, and should rightfully go there again!

Ann Lee's scheming religion is not only treasonous, it is also aimed at breaking up life as we know it! She causes husbands and wives to part! She is responsible for the dissolving of society in peaceful neighborhoods!

Some of the women Shakers strip naked in the woods, thinking they are angels and invisible, and can go about among men and not be seen!

I am convinced the spirit which prevails over this new scheme is the spirit of witchcraft! . . . Ann Lee is Satan in the guise of a sweet angel of light. . . . As the Devil himself at first deceived the woman and made use of her to delude the man, so is he playing once again his old prank by sending us this woman, Ann Lee. . . .

In the midst of this country's great decay of religion and virtue, Ann Lee and her Elders play their magic games. . . . and try to bring the whole creation of man to trial.

The scheme of that self-styled Female Christ, Ann Lee, is so naked that every rational mind should recoil at the thought of falling in with it! Yet multitudes have done so. . . .

And when people are so easily and erroneously carried away, it bespeaks their abysmal ignorance of the truth. MAY GOD PRESERVE YOU!

Valentine Rathbun, Minister of the Gospel,
the public's REAL friend and humble servant!

A quarter of a century later, Shaker Thomas Brown also left the Society. He said he "got hold of the wrong chain." Brown wrote a book, published in 1812, called *An Account of the People Called Shakers.* In it he said that he asked the aged Mary Hocknell about the report that in Mother's day men and women danced naked together. Her somewhat confusing answer was: "Because the brethren pulled off their coats, or outside garments, to labour — or as the world calls it — dance; and in warm weather the sisters being lightly clothed, they would report we danced naked. And you know how apt the ignorant and vulgar parts of mankind are to misrepresent what they see. If one told they danced part naked, or with but few clothes on, another in telling the story, would leave out the part, or few, and so it was reported, obviously, we danced naked."

Even after death, Mother Ann remained a hotly contested figure. Another violent attack was launched upon her by an obviously unbalanced woman named Mary Marshall Dyer, whose tirade makes that of the Reverend Valentine Rathbun sound mild.

The Dyers, with their three children, joined the United Society of Believers in 1811, twenty-seven years after Mother Ann had "dropped her body and gone to heaven." After four years, Mary Marshall Dyer became disenchanted with Shakerism and left. She then sued the Shakers for taking away her husband, her children, and her property.

Mary Marshall Dyer devoted herself to writing lurid pamphlets about them. She charged that "the Shaker spirit is magnetism mingled with sexual passion." She insisted that the Believers were obsessed by sex. Possibly her charge contained a grain of truth. It could be argued that the Shakers' fierce rejection of "carnal nature" indicated a preoccupation with it.

Much of Mary Marshall Dyer's venom was directed toward the founder, Mother Ann, whom she never saw. In a libelous onslaught titled *The Rise and Progress of the Serpent from the Garden of Eden*, she accused the founder of the Shakers of being a fortune-teller, a prostitute, and a drunk. She quoted Mother Ann as saying, "Rum was the Spirit of God, and one of his good creatures," and added that the leader "made much use of it, as did her followers, but after Ann Lee's death, drunkenness abated." Dyer's book, published in 1822, was printed and distributed at her own expense.

The suggestion that alcohol played an important part in the early days of Shakerism seems totally incompatible with the rigorous discipline of the early Believers. Some of the Shaker songs may have contributed to the accusation that Mother Ann was a drinker, though it seems apparent that the intoxicant referred to in verse is religious ecstasy, not alcohol. One song, for example, praises "Mother's wine."

> *Drink ye of Mother's wine,*
> *Drink drink drink ye freely,*
> *Drink ye of Mother's wine*
> *It will make you limber.*
> *If it makes you reel around,*
> *If it makes you fall down*
> *If it lays you on the floor*
> *Rise and take a little more!*

Both Valentine Rathbun and Mary Marshall Dyer harmed the Shakers' reputation. Dyer, however, indulged in such verbal overkill that she defeated her own purpose. She accused Mother Ann of having little children stripped naked and whipped, strung up by their wrists, left alone all night in the woods, even beaten to death. Even people who disliked the Shakers refused to believe Mother Ann would abuse a child. Mary Marshall Dyer lost her lawsuit against the Society. The verdict was that she had attempted to "cast a stigma on the Shakers which they did not deserve."

Perhaps at the bottom of the angry attacks by Shaker enemies lay cold, clammy fear. Since the Believers were utterly convinced that they were in touch with supernatural powers, their peculiar worship, their singing and dancing and visions, may have frightened people. In a day when the world was full of unexplainable events, many people were superstitious. Why was the sun suddenly eclipsed? Why did so many babies die? Why did lightning burn up a house? Why did an epidemic destroy a community? Who knew the answers?

An extraordinarily eloquent, doubt-free woman living in the forest and communing with spirits must have seemed threatening. As Martin Luther said in an earlier, but equally superstitious day, "Many demons are in woods, in waters, in wildernesses, and in dark, pooly places."

One reply to the bitter attacks by Shaker enemies is the indisputable fact that Mother Ann attracted to her new religion many men and women of the highest character and intelligence. She taught them, and embodied in her own life, precepts of honesty, hard work, cleanliness, and thrift that are totally incompatible with the kind of excesses of which she was accused.

During her life she insisted that Shakerism should be judged by its achievements. She stood firm on the biblical precept, "By their fruits ye shall know them." And through all vicissitudes, Mother Ann stressed the power of love, repeating over and over: "God is love, and if you love God, you will love one another." One of the Shaker hymns tells how her people responded to her lead:

> *Love, love, is a blessing*
> *It is worth possessing —*
> *Mother's love is precious and pure,*
> *So I will labor for love, love, love,*
> *Mother's love will always endure.*

Chapter Thirteen

More Love, Sister!
More Love, Brother!

Learn not to be the masters
but the mothers of the souls
entrusted to your care.

— Saint Bernard of Clairvaux
(1090–1154)
A founder
of the Cistercian Order

"You must not lose one minute of your time," Mother Ann would tell her disciples, "for you have none to spare." When she decided, in the spring of 1781, to travel through the northeast to spread the Shaker faith, it was true that her time was valuable. Although just forty-five, she had only three years to live.

For Mother Ann, taking Shakerism "to the world" was urgent because she *knew* the "survival unit" was the whole human race. She often spoke of the "corporate nature of becoming" and declared there could be no such thing as individual salvation since "we are all members one of another."

Accompanied by five of her disciples, she set out from Niskeyuna in May 1781 to journey through Massachusetts and Connecticut, proclaiming the Testimony. With her were her brother, now called Father William, Elder James Whittaker, Samuel Fitch, Margaret Leland, and the ever-faithful Mary Partington. They were to be gone two years on what *Testimonies* calls both "a triumphal tour and a march to the cross."

The six missionaries, eager to share "the gifts of God" with the world's people, stopped first at Tucconock Mountain in the Berkshires. During their ten-day visit, they had their first encounter with an angry mob — again according to *Testimonies*:

> Great power of God, with much manifestation of the power of the spirit upon the physical body, attended the Testimony, as was usual where ever Mother Ann ministered.
>
> This was also followed by much opposition. One Doctor Hollebert attempted to dispute with the Elders, but being confounded and put to the blush by Elder James Whittaker, he went and advised the mob to let them alone; so no acts of violence were committed.

This pattern was to be repeated many times during Mother Ann's New England journey. As the Shaker missionaries went from town to town, their religious fervor aroused enthusiasm among some people but bitter antagonism among others. And they did not always find a Doctor Hollebert to turn away the belligerent crowd.

By now Mother Ann had gained a wide reputation. Men and women, old and young, came in droves

Opposite: A modern map showing Mother Ann's journeys, made by P. Ross Teller in 1952. Courtesy of The Shaker Museum and Library, Old Chatham, New York.

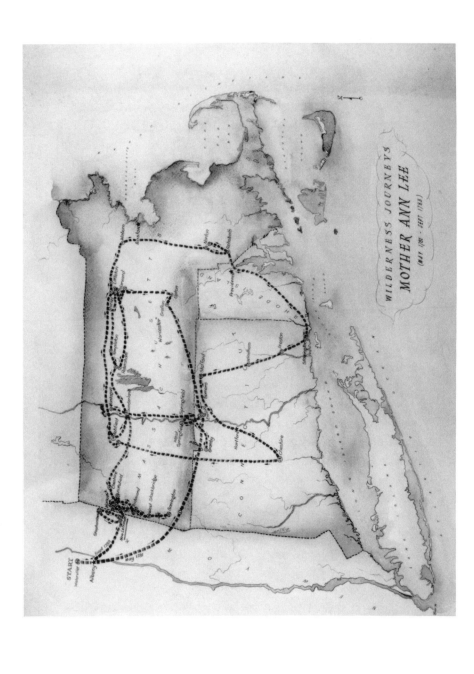

WILDERNESS JOURNEYS
MOTHER ANN LEE
(MAY 1781 - SEPT 1783)

to hear her and to quiz her. Life on the frontier was tense and uncertain and people were captivated by this woman's unwavering conviction that she had found God. She seemed to entertain no doubts whatsoever.

Tirelessly, she preached about self-denial, confession of sin, rejection of the world and the flesh, and pursuit of the Spirit in private prayer and communal worship. "Labor to make the way of God your own," she told them. "Let it be your inheritance, your treasure, your occupation, your daily calling. Labor to God for your own soul as though there was no other creature on earth."

Despite the war raging in the colonies, Mother Ann preached nonresistance and love of the enemy. This infuriated many. She often quoted from the Book of Proverbs, "A soft answer turneth away wrath," and she had ample opportunity to prove her point. *A Summary View* says:

> Every evil report and every wicked device . . . were called forth to calumniate and debase the character of Mother Ann and her companions, and render them odious in the eyes of the people. . . .
>
> The charges of being enemies and traitors to the country; of having fire arms and munitions of war concealed among them; of living in drunkenness and debauchery, and practicing witchcraft and other base crimes, were continually alleged against them.

The Shakers not only met hostility with soft answers, they used music as well. They would have agreed with William Congreve, the English dramatist who wrote, "Music hath charms to soothe the savage breast, to soften rocks, or bend a knotted oak." To the Shakers, music, the universal language, was one of God's most magical gifts.

They did part singing, complicated, rhythmic, and always without accompaniment. They sang wherever they went — songs of greetings and songs of farewell, ritual songs, "gift" songs, dance songs, hymns, and anthems. They taught many of their songs to the people they visited. Being unschooled in how to write music, the Believers developed their own system of notation, using the first seven letters of the alphabet instead of notes. Riding along the dusty roads of New England, they improvised simple songs, such as:

Oh, the gospel of Mother
What blessing it brings
Of substance not obtained
In earthly things.

Mother Ann loved the singing. Once she leaned from her carriage and called to the men following on horseback, "Brethren, be comfortable! Brethren, be joyful!"

"We will, Mother," they answered. And *Testimonies* adds: "Singing joyfully, they arrived at David Green's."

They sang even when they were mistreated. Once when James Whittaker was being beaten by an angry mob in Shirley, Massachusetts, *Testimonies* says, "Elder James had a new song of praise put into his mouth." And in the midst of vicious persecution, Father William Lee composed a wordless tune that became famous among Shakers as "Father William's Dove Song."

Father William's voice was "melodious and powerful" and his songs were described by the Believers as "seeming like music from some superior being." In his book on the Shakers, Thomas Brown said that Father William was always seeking "to praise the Lord with dance and song." Moreover, he had difficulty giving Mother Ann's "soft answer." Once while he was preaching, a youth in the crowd made fun of him.

> Lee took him by the throat and shook him, saying, "When I was in England, I was sergeant in the King's lifeguard, and could then use my fists; but now, since I have received the gospel, I must patiently bear all abuse, and suffer my shins to be kicked by every little boy. But I will have you know that the power of God will defend our cause."

The Shaker missionaries reached Harvard, Massachusetts, by the end of June 1781. Mother Ann liked the peaceful village above the Nashua River with Mount Wachusett in the distance. When she saw the Square House at the end of town, surrounded by green meadows and dark pine forests, she announced it was the place she had seen in her visions in England. This is where they would stay.

It was said that the Shakers "never saw a stranger." Mother Ann often quoted from the thirteenth chapter of Hebrews, "Be not forgetful to entertain strangers, for thereby some have entertained angels unawares." Clara Endicott Sears's book, *Gleanings from Old Shaker Journals,* recounts the story of how the Shakers managed to move themselves in with their new-found friends at the Square House.

Father William spoke to Abigail Cooper, who was living in the Square House with Abigail Lougee.

"Are you willing we should come into your house?"

"No, I don't know as I am," Abigail Cooper replied.

(Previous to this Abigail had gotten a little hint they were going to try to get in at the Square House to make their home there. Knowing they were English people, her feelings were not favorable to them.)

"Well, you'll let us come in, will you?"

"I suppose I must."

They came in and after taking their seats, Mother Ann said, "All we want is to help souls to God."

"I have seen a great deal of false religion," replied Abigail, "and I don't want to see anymore. If you have a new religion you can keep it to yourselves, for all of me."

Mother Ann, looking at one of the Abigails, said, "I have seen you before." Looking around at the rest, she said, "I have seen all of you before."

Mother Ann asked Abigail if she loved them and Abigail said she did not. Then Father William handed Abigail an apple and said, "We will make you love us before we leave the place."

Abigail later said, "I did not want the apple but I took it. Before long I could say in truth I did love them. I loved the apple they gave me, for their sakes. When I was about my work I would look at the apple, and take it in my hand. I knew there was something good about them because I loved them, and I was thankful to take them in, and glad to do anything for them that I could do."

Abigail Lougee's home was called the Square House because of its unusual square roof. It was a roomy, well-built place, just right for big meetings. (The original house is gone now, but the stone steps, huge maples, and stone walls remain.) The house had formerly belonged to an eccentric Baptist preacher named Shadrack Ireland, who had died just before the Shakers arrived.

A disciple of George Whitefield, Ireland was a religious fanatic with quite a following of his own. Unlike the Shakers, he believed in marriage — with a difference. He had left his wife and children in Charlestown and moved into the Square House with his "spiritual bride," Abigail Lougee. Ireland's hidden life with his soulmate must have made him uneasy because he built a cupola on the roof and spent hours up there watching to see if anyone was coming.

Unlike the Shakers, Shadrack Ireland believed, literally, in physical life after death. He told his followers *if* he died at all, he would certainly come back on the third day. He did die — and Abigail Lougee, believing he was not really dead, refused to have him buried. She and her friend Abigail Cooper were sure Shadrack would return to life. They spent days and nights eagerly waiting beside his body, but he remained cold and stark. At last they could stand it no longer. Abigail Lougee had the Reverend Ireland placed in a coffin and had the coffin bricked up in the Square House cellar.

According to records kept by the Harvard Shakers, Mother Ann had not lived in the Square House long before she was awakened in the night by a spine-chilling visitation from Ireland's phantom . She got up, woke everyone in the house, and called a meeting. "We must all pray for the power of God," she said, "for there are the darkest spirits here that I ever sensed. Shadrack Ireland is *here*. He began in the spirit and ended in the most total darkness of the flesh."

Mother and all her people went "into the labors, or danced" to dispel Shadrack's sinister spirit. No ghost was a match for Mother's zeal, and Shadrack Ireland's spirit must surely have been exorcised from the Square House that night.

Early records show that the Shakers bought the Square House, that Mother Ann contributed $144.17 toward the purchase, and that Mother Ann personally converted Shadrack's "spiritual wife," Abigail Lougee, to Shakerism.

Mother was able to persuade Abigail Lougee that the body was not immortal. "The evidence of the senses," she told her, "makes the claim ridiculous." She lectured Ireland's followers on the subject.

You are old people now, all of you, and you think you shall never die. Look at yourselves! *You* carry about you all the marks of mortality, just as other people do. Your skins are wrinkled; your hair turns white and is falling; your eyesight is failing; you are losing your teeth and your bodies are growing feeble. How inconsistent to think you shall never die. All natural bodies must die and turn to dust! *Repent*, for the Kingdom of God is at hand!

Soon the Square House was the center of a whirling vortex of religious enthusiasts seeking salvation. Hundreds of men and women came there to be converted and to learn Shaker worship. Mother Ann said worship was changing the set of a person's mind, and this she knew how to do. Her exhortations brought forth joyous shouts and mournful wailings that were heard all over town.

"Love that power!" cried Mother Ann when the "gift of shaking" seized the converts. "It is the shaking of the dry bones, to bring bone to its bone." Even people who were not sure what she meant were affected by Mother's vibrations. As the dancing and singing reached a crescendo, she would shout, "More love, Brother! More love, Sister!"

It is not surprising that a woman whose motto was "Do all the good you can, in all the ways you can, as often as you can, to all the people you can" would attract others. All kinds of people came to Mother Ann for help. One woman tottered in weeping because her swollen legs were so painful. Mother Ann, who must have had the power to reduce anxiety, placed her hands upon her and soon the woman's legs were cured. No wonder she said of Mother Ann, "Her smile was like sunshine."

Many others spoke of Mother Ann's infectious smile and laugh. She enjoyed a joke, and she was utterly without pretense. When a visitor complimented her on her unusual humility, she replied, "I always admired pride — in a horse." Mother's humor was kindly. A Shaker maxim, handed down from the early days, may have originated with her: "Jests and jokes are edged tools, and very dangerous to use, as they wound the tender feelings of our friends."

Not everyone in Harvard, Massachusetts, appreciated Mother Ann. One day a "spoiled girl" named

Jemima Blanchard came to the Square House to confess that she had been telling everybody that Mother Ann was a witch. Mother took Jemima by the hand and said, "I forgive you, and pray God to forgive you. There is no witchcraft but sin."

Soon after that, Jemima Blanchard, entirely against her parents' wishes, "put away her sins and became a child of God." The young convert must have found Shakerism highly exhilarating because *Testimonies* says: "Jemima would sometimes go from the Square House to the South House, whirling rapidly and passing over fences, or whatever came in her way, without touching them or making the least effort to clear them. At times she would be entirely supported by the power without touching any material thing."

While the Shakers were in residence in the Square House, a wild rumor began to spread that the world was coming to an end. Every generation seems to confront this fear at one time or another. People came to Mother Ann for protection because they were terrified that "the end" was near. She had no time for such frenzy. Over and over, she told them she was not concerned with the end of the world. "I am only concerned," Mother Ann said firmly, "with the end of *worldliness*."

Chapter Fourteen

Is She Really a Woman?

Anatomy is destiny.

— Sigmund Freud

Celibate societies have appeared throughout religious history, but only the Shakers required chastity of males and females living in a closely knit community. Shakers even expected celibacy of Believers who once were husband and wife. This extraordinary way of life ignited indignation and anger in others. People refused to believe that men and women, working intimately together, could abstain from sexual contact of any kind. To many, the whole concept was repugnant.

Issachar Bates's autobiography records some of the accusations that were leveled at Shakers by their critics. "The very air and woods," wrote Bates, "rung with the appalling sound of False Prophets! Seducers! Deceivers! Liars! Wolves in sheep's clothing! Parting man and wife! Breaking up families and churches!"

He describes the relish with which village gossips circulated rumors that Believers castrated their males, danced naked during night meetings, and indulged in perverted debauchery. It was even said that babies born of their unlawful embraces were secretly murdered. Although Bates calls this vicious talk "croaking of bullfrogs," the wild rumors undoubtedly inflamed the prejudice already smouldering around the Shakers.

Mother Ann was the lightning rod that attracted most of the wrath. When she exhorted in her vivid language against sexual lust and the sins of the flesh, hostile crowds insulted her. One Shaker historian commented sardonically: "The fact of a woman presuming to preach and teach against the natural life, against the good Bible command *to multiply and replenish the earth,* was cause for decisive action. No matter if the earth were already replenished to repletion, 'til actual starvation threatened themselves and their children with death; that command they would adhere to, no matter what others were broken."

"Decisive action" of the most deplorable kind is what Mother Ann was subjected to one bitter December night in the Massachusetts village of Petersham. After she established the Shaker leaders in the Square House, she had left Harvard to take the Testimony to the neighboring towns of ·Shirley, Littleton, Woburn, and Petersham.

Word spread that Mother Ann was a "virago," a derogatory term for "a woman who had masculine qualities of mind and body." Some said she was not a woman at all; she was a man dressed up like a woman. Certainly, she was unlike any woman ever seen in Petersham. Several tough characters in the town decided to kidnap her, so they could examine her and find out for sure if she were a male or a female. *Testimonies* tells the whole shocking, shameful story. The careful attention to detail gives the saga a ring of authenticity.

> This being the first visit that Mother Ann and the Elders made in Petersham the inhabitants generally manifested a desire to see and hear her for themselves, and as they pretended civility, they had full liberty.
>
> Accordingly, on Monday evening there came a considerable number of civil people, also a company of lewd fellows . . . who styled themselves the blackguard committee.
>
> Elder James Whittaker . . . then began to speak . . . the mob had opportunity to arrange themselves through the assembly without being much noticed. Instantly a cry was heard, "Knock out the lights!"
>
> The lights were all suddenly extinguished, except the one in Elder James's hand. . . . At this instant entered three ruffians painted black, and rushing forward, the foremost one seized hold of Mother, and, with the assistance of his comrades, attempted to drag her out, but Elizabeth Shattuck and several other sisters instantly clinched hold of her, and held her, and Elizabeth being a large, heavy woman, and the passage narrow, the ruffians were not able to accomplish their purpose; and quitting their hold they suddenly fled out of the house.
>
> In this struggle . . . they tore a breadth out of a new gown which Mother had on. Their wicked design being now fully known, Elder James advised to have the remainder of the assembly withdraw.

But Mother, in the spirit of prophecy, said the wicked would come again. . . . However, as the mob had withdrawn and all danger apparently at an end, the neighboring Believers returned home. . . .

Those who remained were about retiring to rest when Mother discovered from the window, that her cruel persecutors were near, and made some attempts to conceal herself. The house was again assaulted by about thirty creatures in human shape; the doors, being fastened, were burst open and broke, and these ruffians entered. . . .

Elder James Whittaker was clinched by the collar, knocked down and left for dead; and several others were knocked down. Father William Lee was also hurt, and all who stood in their way were beaten and bruised. . . .

As their object was to seize Mother Ann, the candles had been previously concealed to prevent their finding her. But this did not hinder them; they seized fire brands, and searched the house, and at length, found her in a bedroom; they immediately seized her by the feet, and inhumanly dragged her, feet foremost, out of the house, and threw her into a sleigh with as little ceremony as they would the dead carcass of a beast, and drove off, committing, at the same time, acts of inhumanity and indecency which even savages would be ashamed of.

In the struggle with these inhuman wretches, she lost her cap and handkerchief, and otherwise had her clothes torn in a shameful manner. Their pretense was to find out whether she was a woman or not.

In this situation, in a cold winter's night, they drove nearly three miles to Samuel Peckham's tavern, near Petersham Meetinghouse. Father William Lee feeling great concern for Mother's safety, he and David Hammond followed the sleigh.

He told the ruffians that she was his sister and he would follow her; and, attempting to hold on to the hind part of the sleigh, they gave him many blows with the butts of their sleigh whips. . . .

It appeared that Samuel Peckham was a Captain of militia, and had previously agreed with the ruffians who seized Mother, to give them as much rum as they would drink, on condition that they would bring her to his house.

After they arrived Father William Lee and David Hammond remonstrated against the ungodliness and brutality of their behavior. David presented to them the unlawfulness of such conduct, and how they had exposed themselves to the penalties of the law.

Being by this time ashamed of their conduct, and fearful of the consequences, they promised to release Mother Ann upon condition that David would sign an obligation not to prosecute them for what they had done. Being impelled by a feeling for Mother's safety, he reluctantly yielded to their demands, and left them to answer at the bar of Divine justice. . . .

This being done, they released Mother Ann, and some time in the night some of them brought her and those with her back to David Hammond's.

She came in singing for joy that she was again restored to her children [meaning her spiritual followers]. The men who brought her back appeared to be greatly ashamed of their wicked conduct, and confessed that they had abused her shamefully, said they were sorry for it, and desired her forgiveness. Mother Ann replied, "I can freely forgive you, I hold nothing against you, and I pray God to forgive you"; so they departed peaceably. . . .

Elder James Whittaker, who had been prevented from following Mother by reason of the severe wound which he had received, informed her of his abuses. His face was greatly swollen, and his jaw very painful, and he was apprehensive that it was broken; but, said he, "I can pray for them," and kneeling down, he cried, "Father, forgive them, for they know not what they do."

Mother Ann's capacity to forgive those who tortured her seems superhuman. How could she say, "I hold nothing against you" to louts who had violated her person? Years before, when the mob had tried to stone her to death in England, she had been able declare: "I felt myself completely surrounded by God's presence and my soul was filled with love." Clearly, Mother Ann possessed extraordinary power, derived perhaps from her obedience to the instructions that Saint Paul gave the early Christians in Rome (Romans 12:19–21), *Dearly beloved, avenge not yourselves, but rather give place unto wrath: for it is written, Vengeance is mine; I will repay, saith the Lord. Therefore if thine enemy hunger, feed him; if he thirst, give him drink: for in so doing thou shalt heap coals of fire on his head. Be not overcome of evil, but overcome evil with good.*

Perhaps Mother Ann's praying for the hoodlums who had captured her and explored her anatomy did indeed "heap coals of fire" on their heads. A person who

The stone marker on the spot where the Shakers were beaten. Note the misspelling of whipped. Courtesy of Fruitlands Museum, Harvard, Massachusetts.

is able to forgive a grave injustice gains great power. Mother Ann often used this power of forgiveness to try to awaken wrongdoers to the Christ Spirit that she believed lay within each of them. Although Mother's forgiveness did not always subdue her enemies, it had an enduring effect on her followers, and is reflected in many of the Shaker songs :

> *I love Mother,*
> *I love her power,*
> *I know it 'twill*
> *Help me in every trying hour,*
> *Help me to shake up,*
> *Help me to break up,*
> *Help me to shake up,*
> *Every bond and fetter.*

While Mother Ann was away on her missionary travels, goings-on at the Square House alarmed the townspeople of Harvard. As in the witchcraft hysteria in Salem a century earlier, fear was followed by panic and destruction. The first indication that there was going to be trouble came when a company of militia-men forced their way into the Shakers' house on the pretext of searching for "a large cache of arms intended for the British." They found nothing, of course, but the Brethren who tried to keep the soldiers out of the sisters' quarters were bruised and bloodied.

Then on a hot morning in August, hideous violence erupted. Before dawn a mob surrounded the Square House. Armed with horsewhips and clubs, they had come to drive the Shakers out of town. As the mob charged into the house, the Believers knelt to pray for

God's protection. Their prayers were cut short. The thugs dragged them into the street, some by the throat, some by the hair.

Then the cruel march began. The Shakers were driven like cattle ten miles, from Harvard to Lancaster, in a horrifying display of brutality. Old people were beaten as they struggled to keep up. Men and women who prayed aloud were whipped across the face. For "a little diversion," the marchers stopped to torture James Shepard, the only one in the group who had come from England with Mother Ann.

As they stripped Father James to the waist, he turned to the other Believers and said, "Be of good cheer, Brethren and Sisters, for it is your Heavenly Father's good pleasure to give you the Kingdom." The others had to watch helplessly while Father James was scourged until "his back was all in a gore of blood and the flesh bruised to a jelly."

Some Shakers tried to cover him with their bodies. They, too, were horsewhipped. William Morey — "a zealous Believer who denounced the ruffians for abusing the defenseless" — had his teeth knocked out. With blood streaming from his mouth, Morey shouted at the mob, trying to stop them, to no avail.

When the gruesome parade finally reached Lancaster, the "distant brethren" were banished to Niskeyuna, with a warning never to return. The local converts were herded back to town over the same weary miles. On the leafy road beside the Pollard house, near the spot where Father James had been horsewhipped, a Harvard Shaker named Abijah Worster was tied to a sycamore tree and beaten on his bare back. He was accused of "going about breaking up churches and families."

That historic sycamore tree, with its gigantic cream-colored trunk, is still standing, its heart-shaped leaves spread above the many-windowed house that once belonged to Thaddeus Pollard. A stone memorial nearby bears a sad inscription: *On this spot a Shaker was whiped* [sic] *by a mob for religious views in 1783.*

At the end of that infamous day, as they straggled toward home, the Shakers were bleeding and weak, but uncowed. They sang songs of praise to God. They gave thanks that, like heroes in the Bible, they were deemed worthy of suffering persecution for the sake of their faith.

Why did the gentle Shakers incur murderous anger wherever they went? Perhaps others considered their way of life — so God centered, so loving, so disciplined and dedicated — a criticism of their own lives. We know that injury to a person's self-esteem often produces aggression. When normal human beings, filled with normal self-concern and greed, witnessed the Shakers' valiant attempts to reform the human spirit, fury may have been inevitable. As one early Shaker record book expressed it: "Such genuine marks of Christianity were too much for the seed of Cain to endure."

Mobs continued to pursue Mother Ann and the Elders as they made their way back to Niskeyuna. When they reached New Lebanon, they felt as if they were almost home. Yet soon after their arrival, the redoubtable Mother Ann was dragged into court again.

While Judge Eleazer Grant watched, unconcerned, the constable attacked Mother with his staff. He gave her a severe blow across her breast, probably aimed at discovering whether or not she was a woman. Mother Ann turned to the judge and said, "It is your day now, but it will be mine, by and by. Eleazer Grant, I'll put you into a cockleshell yet." *Testimonies* records that Mother Ann carried the mark of that blow on her breast the rest of her life.

After a bond had been posted, the judge allowed Mother Ann to go free — but a mob prevented her from getting into her carriage. Judge Grant's callousness gives us a picture of the prevailing attitude toward a female in the eighteenth century who dared to lead. He came to the door and said, "As magistrate of the state of New York, I desire that there be no mobs, nor riots." Then he added slyly, "Lay your hands on no man." *Testimonies* says: "These words he repeated several times, laying a peculiar emphasis on the last words, *no man*." The judge disappeared into the building and was seen no more that day. The mob took his words as a license "to abuse Mother at their pleasure, seeing she was a woman." This they did until some Brethren came to her aid.

Miraculously, Mother Ann survived the tribulations and torments of her trip "to the world," but it took a toll. Her robust health was broken. By the time the travelers reached the ferry opposite Albany, she was weak with fatigue. Her extraordinary stamina was gone forever. A number of Indians were at the ferry, and when they saw Mother Ann drive up in her carriage they cried out, "The Good Woman is come! The Good Woman is come!" Having endured so much abuse, Mother must have found comfort in the warmth and friendliness of the Indians.

She and the Elders ferried across the broad Hudson and proceeded until they entered a forest northwest of Albany. There they stopped to rest and watch the autumn sun set. Some wanted to stay overnight, but Mother Ann was eager to return to the Shaker colony she loved so much. They journeyed on, finally arriving at Niskeyuna late at night.

They had been gone two years and four months, traveled hundreds of miles, and suffered indescribable hardship and persecution. Mother Ann had introduced The United Society of Believers in Christ's Second Appearing into many communities. She founded Shaker societies in six new places: New Lebanon in New York; Enfield in Connecticut; and Hancock, Harvard, Shirley, and Tyringham in Massachusetts. She did not get as far north as Maine and New Hampshire. The Shaker colonies that flourished in those two states were established after she died.

Mother Ann started on her New England journey during the dark days of the American Revolution. Soon after she returned to Niskeyuna, Lord Cornwallis surrendered to General Washington at Yorktown. On October 19,1781, what America's friend the English statesman William Pitt termed "a most accursed, wicked, barbarous, cruel, unnatural, unjust, and diabolical war" came to an end. Eight long, bitter years after a ragged volley was fired at Lexington Green, America had won its independence.

The Shakers took no part in the Revolutionary War, nor would they take part in any other war. Their record of complete pacifism remained untarnished. Throughout those eight bloody years of revolution, they labored with single-minded zeal to establish in America The United Society of Believers in Christ's Second Appearing.

After the Americans defeated the British, Mother Ann — dedicated pacifist though she was — knelt in thanks to God. She knew too well the power of oppression. She would have agreed whole-heartedly with the Marquis de Lafayette's oft-quoted remark: "I have always loved liberty with the enthusiasm of a religious man, with the passion of a lover, and with the conviction of a geometrician." She must have been encouraged, too, about the possibility of the Millennium. The Millennium is defined in the earliest Shaker manifesto (1808) as a time when "all tyrannical and oppressive governments shall be overthrown and destroyed, and mankind enjoy just and equal rights in all matters, civil and religious."

When Lord Cornwallis surrendered to General Washington at Yorktown, the band played "The World Turned Upside Down." When Mother Ann was asked why Shaker values were so different from the world's values, she had replied, "We are the people who turned the world upside down." Each in his own way — American Shaker and American soldier — were part of the great unending drama of a dedicated people trying to establish a free nation under God.

Chapter Fifteen

The Death
of Mother Ann

How much they are deceived,
Who think that Mother's dead!
She lives among her offspring,
Who just begin to spread . . .

— Shaker Spiritual

There are two ways to be rich. One is to have a lot of money; the other is to have very few needs. Mother Ann, the child of the Manchester slums who grew up in poverty, dedicated herself to simplicity of life. She eschewed earthly possessions in order to consecrate her life to God and she taught the Shakers that thrift was sacred. "Nothing ever runs out of use," she told them, "an item or a person."

Dressed only in homespun, Mother called for "plainness in all things." She told her followers, "You may let the moles and bats — that is, the children of this world — have the gold beads, jewels, and silver buckles. They set their hearts upon such things but the people of God do not want them." For her it was far more important to nourish the spirit than nourish the body. *A*

Summary View says, "When occasion required, she would cheerfully make her meal on the fragments left by others, and say, ' This is good enough for me, for it is the blessing of God, and must not be lost.' "

By the beginning of 1784, much to the distress of her followers, it was clear that Mother Ann's life was "running out of use." As her days dwindled down, she began to tell her children how to take care of things after she was gone. She laid great stress on their stewardship of God's earth, especially on cultivating the land "to yield her increase and develop her beauty." This must be done, she told them, in a spirit of love because "the earth yields most to those who love it." The Believers did as Mother directed, bestowing on the gardens and fields of Niskeyuna the attention that others bestow on material possessions.

Having known so much privation, Mother Ann was appalled by waste. "You must be prudent and saving of every good thing that God blesses you with," she said, "so that you may have wherewith to give to them that stand in need. You cannot make a spear of grass nor a kernel of grain grow, if you know you must die for the want of it. It is by the blessing of God that these things come: therefore you ought not to waste the least thing."

After her turbulent trip through New England, Mother Ann never recovered her health. Her once strong body grew increasingly weaker and she knew her days were numbered. *Testimonies* says, "Mother sat in a chair almost all day and sang in unknown tongues the whole time, and seemed to be wholly divested of any attention to material things."

It is easy to imagine her rocking and singing in her primitive chair, which is now displayed at Fruitlands Museums in Harvard, Massachusetts. A seven-rung Windsor chair with wide rockers fastened to the legs, it is a crude forerunner of the exquisitely simple chairs for which later Shakers became famous.

As the news of Mother's failing health spread, many came to visit her at Niskeyuna. One of them wrote, "All sat on the floor on a carpet of Mother's love, soft as velvet. She lectured to the adoring Believers on the importance of work-as-worship. Labor, she said, was sacred. She had told her disciple Calvin Harlow: "Before you become a great preacher of The Word, you will first have to get out and learn how to do manual labor." And she told her visitors, "When you return home you must be diligent with your hands. . . . The Devil tempts others, but an idle person tempts the Devil. When you are at work, doing your duty as a gift to God, the Devil can have no power over you, because there is no room for temptation."

Also high on Mother Ann's list of priorities was cleanliness. "Good spirits do not live where there is dirt," she declared. "There *is* no dirt in heaven." One woman who came was amazed by the cleanliness, order, and simplicity she found at the Shaker settlement. "Though I was brought up in New England among good farmers," she said, "I never saw such neatness and economy as was here displayed in the wilderness."

Order in all things was Mother Ann's credo. She said it was "the creator of beauty and the protection of souls." But the order she cared most about was interior order. "You must first establish order within yourself," she said. The true source of unhappiness, according to Mother, was the incoherence in people's lives caused by barrenness and confusion within.

Saint Augustine said he was a question to himself. For the dying Mother Ann there were no questions. Years before, she had tackled the immense, seemingly impossible, task of totally remaking herself. This she achieved with invincible fortitude, cutting away all of her personal desires in order to reach God. Her concentration on her goal seemed to fulfill the biblical prophecy that "when the eye is single, the whole body is full of light."

She was able to face her own death with equanimity. She said she had confronted the dark tides within herself and was now in touch with the deepest part of her being where there were pools of harmony and peace.

Not surprisingly, given her mystical temperament, Mother Ann had a premonition of her own death. When the Elders and Elderesses were planning for the future, she would say, "You may live to see it, but I shall not." She forecast the opening of Shaker communities in the southwest where "there will be a great work of God." Eventually, Shakerism did spread into Ohio, Kentucky, and Indiana, where it lasted for nearly a hundred years.

She often spoke about her approaching death in parables. Like Jesus, she knew that the best way to teach is to tell a story. *Testimonies* tells how she gazed at a heavily laden apple tree and said to Sister Hannah, "How beautiful this tree is now! But some of the apples will soon fall off; some will hold on longer. Some will hold on till they are half grown, and then fall off, and some will get ripe. So it is with souls who set out in the way of God. Many will set out very fair, and soon fall away; some will go further, and then fall off; some will go further still, and then fall; and some will go through."

One of the Sisters, Eunice Goodrich, who was apparently not given to understatement, said, "So great was the manifestation of the power of God in Mother Ann at this time that many were unable to abide in her presence. Her words were like flames of fire, and her voice like peals of thunder, and her countenance beautiful and glorious."

While Mother Ann was able to contemplate her own death calmly, she found it excruciating to watch the deterioration of her younger brother, once so handsome and strong. In his military days, William Lee had been skilled in "pugilistic arts," and after he joined the Shakers his ability to do hard work was legendary. Once after shoeing a horse he asked the owner of the smithy what he owed. "Nothing," the man replied. "If a man can work like that, it is pay enough to watch him." Now, at the age of forty-four, William was feeble and ill. On a summer's day, he asked one of the brothers to sing to him, and while he was listening to the music, Father William "passed into the world of the spirit." The date was July 21, 1784.

Father William was the first of the original English group to die. The cause of his death is not clear. *Testimonies* says, "He did not appear to die by any natural infirmity; but seemed to give up his life in sufferings." Mother Ann was sure he died as a result of the violence he had endured on their travels, and he did take to the grave the wounds he received defending her.

After her brother's death, Mother Ann's grasp on life grew more tenuous. Although she firmly believed he was enjoying a better life, she was desolate without him. In her beautiful voice, she sang a Shaker hymn:

I know how to pray,
I know how to be thankful,
For God has blessed me
With a broken heart.

From then on, she "continually grew weaker in body," *Testimonies* states, "without any visible appearance of bodily disease." By September, it was apparent that the end was near. Job Bishop, who later founded the first Shaker colony in New Hampshire, recalled hearing her say shortly before her death, "I shall soon be taken out of this body. But the Gospel will never be taken away from you, if you are faithful. Be not discouraged nor cast down; for God will not leave his people without a leader."

Death had no dominion over Mother Ann, for in that ecstatic moment years before when she had the vision in Manchester jail, she surrendered herself completely and unconditionally to God. She had lived the rest of her life "on a wonderful threshold." With her gift for relating the immediate to the infinite, she told her followers, "Live together, every day, as though it was the last you had to live in this world."

During her last days, her words were faithfully recorded by the Believers. To Brother John Barns she said, "You think that you will yet subdue and overcome the nations of the earth, but you are mistaken. The nations will have that work to do for themselves. They will fight and devour, and dash each other to pieces until they become so humble as to be willing to receive the Gospel."

To Sisters Anna Matthewson and Lucy Wright she said, "I see the opening of the heavens, and I see heavens of heavens, as it were, glory beyond glory; and still see that which does excel in glory."

Just before she died, she murmured, "I see my brother William coming in a glorious chariot to take me home."

"And when the breath left her body," *Testimonies* adds, "Elder John Hocknell, who was greatly gifted in visions, testified that . . . he saw a golden chariot drawn by four white horses, which received and wafted her soul out of sight."

She was only forty-eight when she died, but as she said years before, "It is not important how long one has been in the work. What is important is how much work has been done."

Mother Ann's obituary, printed in *The Albany Gazette* on September 9, 1784, read:

Departed this life, at Nisquenia, Sept. 7, Mrs. Lee, known by the appellation of the *Elect Lady* or *Mother of Zion*, and head of that people called Shakers. Her funeral is to be attended this day.

News of her death was carried by messenger to all Shaker "families." Many people, Believers and unbelievers alike, made the journey from Albany to Niskeyuna to attend her burial. Shaker funerals did not recognize grief. The happy transference of the soul from the body to "a fusion of earthly spheres" was a time of inspiration.

Instead of a formal ritual, Mother Ann's followers took turns exhorting others to follow her example. They said Mother could not die and was not dead and had not ceased to live among her people. She had only withdrawn from the common sight. She had cast off the dress of flesh and was now clothed in a glory that concealed her from the world. She, Ann, The Word, the female embodiment of Christ, was transported to a realm where *there is neither bond nor free, there is neither male nor female, for all are one in Christ.*

Father James Whittaker, to whom Mother Ann had passed the lead from her deathbed, said that the union Mother Ann experienced with Christ had given her extraordinary power to draw others to her. If the Believers, like Mother, would cease to cling to the world and the flesh, they too could find that Truth which transforms life. "Be not conformed to this world!" he cried. "But be ye transformed by the perfect will of God!"

Then they all sang spirituals that overflowed with Mother's conviction that the Second Coming is here and now — a miraculous awakening within the heart and mind of each individual. Songs, perhaps, like this Prayer Song which describes the life of Mother Ann Lee:

> *I never did believe*
> *That I ever could be saved*
> *Without giving up All to God.*
> *So I freely give the whole,*
> *My body and my soul,*
> *To the Lord God,*
> *Amen.*

Two of the brethren had dug her grave and two others had made her a wooden coffin "devoid of decoration." Lovingly, they placed the coffin on a wagon and took the body of their beloved founder to the Shaker cemetery. There, near a flowing stream, they buried Mother Ann in a grove of maples and pines. Her plain marble tombstone reads:

MOTHER
ANN LEE
BORN IN MANCHESTER,
ENGLAND.
FEB . 29, 1736.
DIED IN WATERVLIET N.Y.
SEPT. 8, 1784.

Epilogue

Shakerism after Mother Ann

People who venture beyond common concepts — such as the fear of death — and come into the world of the spirit are the true heroes.

— Joseph Campbell: *The Hero with a Thousand Faces*

Mother Ann's spiritual crusade might have perished with her. Her successor, Father James Whittaker, only thirty-three when he assumed the lead, carried on for two years — then, quite suddenly, died. Mother Ann, with her usual foresight, had groomed two other strong leaders who stood ready to take his place.

One was Joseph Meacham, called by Mother her Saint Peter — "the rock upon whom the church was founded." The other was Lucy Wright, of whom Mother said the first time she saw her: "We *must* have that young woman. She will be worth a whole nation." Lucy's husband, Elizur Goodrich, also joined the Shakers; but Lucy, like Ann Lee, kept her own name.

Father Joseph and Mother Lucy were to exceed Mother Ann's high expectations. With energy and skill, they guided and goaded the Society cf Believers in Christ's Second Appearing into success and spread the gospel through New England. By 1800, eleven Shaker communities had been formed.

Since equality was considered essential, the Society was open to all. Mother Rebecca Jackson, one of several black members, led a small Shaker family in Philadelphia — and that was *before* the Civil War. Jews, native Americans, foreigners — all were welcome. In nineteenth-century America, such a total absence of bigotry was revolutionary.

The membership peaked by 1845. At its zenith, there were about six thousand Shakers who held in common ownership more than one hundred thousand acres of land. After that the numbers started declining. But the Shakers never measured their ministry in numbers. Success was a single soul saved. Shaker impact on the world was out of all proportion to their numbers.

Ironically, it was not their spiritual life but their material successes that attracted outside interest in the Shakers. Although the Believers shunned materialism, they were so hard-working, and so thrifty, that almost without realizing what was happening, they became financially successful. Much of their money went into the purchase of land.

Because Shakers believed work is worship, they labored ceaselessly and strove for excellence in all things. Their motto was *Who does his best does well*. They used only the finest materials and produced flawless work. Soon the world was beating a path to their door.

Constance Rourke writes in *The Roots of American Culture*: "Shaker fairness in matters of trade became a byword throughout New England and even their enemies acknowledged that they excelled in mechanical

1	Watervliet, New York	(1787–1938)
2	New Lebanon, New York	(1787–1947)
3	Hancock, Massachusetts	(1790–1960)
4	Enfield, Connecticut	(1790–1917)
5	Tyringham, Massachusetts	(1792–1875)
6	Harvard, Massachusetts	(1791–1918)
7	Shirley, Massachusetts	(1793–1908)
8	Canterbury, New Hampshire	(1792–present)
9	Enfield, New Hampshire	(1793–1923)
10	Alfred, Maine	(1793–1931)
11	Sabbathday Lake, Maine	(1794–present)
12	Gorham, Maine	(1808–1819)
13	Savoy, Massachusetts	(1817–1825)
14	Sodus Bay, New York	(1826–1836)
15	Groveland, New York	(1836–1895)
16	North Union, Ohio	(1822–1889)
17	Union Village, Ohio	(1806–1912)
18	Whitewater, Ohio	(1824–1907)
19	Watervliet, Ohio	(1806–1910)
20	West Union (Busro), Indiana	(1810–1827)
21	Pleasant Hill, Kentucky	(1806–1910)
22	South Union, Kentucky	(1807–1922)
23	White Oak, Georgia	(1898–1902)
24	Narcoossee, Florida	(1896–1911)

A map showing the eventual locations of twenty-four Shaker communities.
Courtesy of Priscilla J. Brewer.

arts." They excelled in the cultivation of herbs, fruits and flowers, and the raising of livestock as well.

Their honesty was equalled by their ingenuity. The Believers were the first to dry seeds and sell them in packets; the first to fashion cut nails and metallic pens; the first to make a four-wheel dump wagon; the first to air-condition beehives (by vents); the first to make permanent-press, water-repellent fabric; the first to weave palm leaf bonnets on a loom; and the first to market herb medicines for the ailing and manuals for the gardener. Who but the Shakers would think of putting a rack to hold a shawl on the back of a rocker, or buttons for "tilting" on the bottom of chair legs, or insulators on irons to hold the heat?

Since Mother Ann had taught them it was important not to overwork, and since their daily work had to be stopped repeatedly for periods of prayer, they applied their wits and their wisdom to making labor-saving devices. Their inventions ranged from the momentous to the minuscule. They invented the flat broom, clothespin, a type of washing machine, circular saw, automatic spring, turbine water wheel, a version of the threshing machine, tongue-and-groove machine (for matching boards), revolving oven (to bake sixty pies at once), apple parer, stove-cover lifter, bread cutter, herb presser, sleeve ironer, spindle bender, table swift (a reel for winding yarn that sold originally for fifty cents and is now a museum item), pea sheller, berry-basket maker, potato peeler, pill dryer, peanut sheller, and a static electricity generator. In all, those ingenious Believers are credited with over forty inventions.

People who came to the communes to trade were dazzled by Shaker cleanliness and order. No spots of dirt or dust were permitted, for Mother Ann had taught them evil spirits live where there is dirt. The extreme neatness of the buildings, fields, gardens, outhouses, and barnyards was almost beyond belief. Outside, firewood was cut and stacked in exact order; inside, only bare essentials were left in sight. Even the chairs were suspended on wall pegs — upside down to keep dust off the seats — so the bare floors could be swept several times a day.

Professor Benjamin Silliman of Yale, one of many nineteenth-century scholars interested in the Shakers, said: "Such neatness and order is not seen anywhere on so large a scale, except in Holland, where it is a necessity. Here it is voluntary."

Working not for gain, but with loving care because their labor brought them closer to God, the Shakers unwittingly created a new style. Aimed at the perfection demanded for eternity, the things they made were to last forever. Their exquisite sense of symmetry sprang from a desire to express "the eternal two " — the male and female duality of the Deity. In crafts, in furniture design, in architecture, they achieved bare-boned simplicity. Because they believed the objects with the greatest usefulness possessed the greatest beauty, their utterly uncluttered creations were utilitarian and minimalist long before those aesthetic ideas had even surfaced.

The pared-down Shaker style, now widely admired and imitated, was too stark for the elaborate Victorians. Charles Nordhoff, a journalist and sociologist who in 1875 published a book on *Communistic Societies of the United States*, expressed admiration for the Shakers, but he was horrified by the severity of their work. "It seeks only the useful," he complained, "and cares nothing for grace and beauty, and carefully avoids ornament." Nordhoff asked one Shaker if they were to build anew, would they aim at "some beauty of design"?

The elder's reply could be the Shaker's aesthetic credo. "No," he said, "The beautiful, as you call it, is absurd and abnormal. It has no business with us. A man has no right to waste money on what you call beauty in his house or his daily life, while there are people living in misery."

Tastes change. Museums and collectors now vie with one another for pieces of Shaker craftsmanship and pay astronomical prices for them. Few today would deny that the Shakers left the "world's people" a legacy of beauty.

There is one facet of Shaker creativity that seems to contradict their stated belief that anything decorative or fanciful is "contrary to order." That is their nineteenth-century inspirational drawings, or "gifts." Some years after Mother Ann's death, the Believers were engulfed by a wave of spiritualism. "The Era of Manifestations," which began at Niskeyuna in 1837 and quickly spread to the other communities, was marked by divine messages from the world of the spirit, some in pictures, some in fine script. These unique spirit drawings became important both as an expression of Shaker faith and as a highly original American folk art.

Symbols abound in the delicate spirit drawings. Apples represent love; pears are for faith; roses for chastity; chains for union and strength; colored balls for comfort, light, and love. Precious jewels and exotic flowers are used to suggest the wondrous "heavenly sphere." Not surprisingly, some of the most exquisite drawings are the "gifts" sent from beyond the grave by

Mother Ann herself. Shaker spiritualism ended in the 1860s and many of the drawings were destroyed. Those that survive are extremely valuable.

The Shaker legacy lives on in the arts — in the sunstruck, angular paintings of Charles Sheeler; in the music of Aaron Copland, whose *Appalachian Spring* echoes the Shakers' "'Tis the Gift To Be Simple"; in the beautiful re-creation of Shaker dance by Martha Graham; in the novel by John Fowles, *A Maggot*, in which Mother Ann Lee insists that "a Holy Trinity that has no female component cannot be holy."

Doris Humphrey, who choreographed Graham's moving ballet, praises Shaker style for its "directness, meticulous structure, immaculate line devoid of super-fluous ornament." She writes admiringly of the unclut-tered rooms in their functional dwellings, their fastidious dress, the austerity and practicality of their lives." Then she adds this insightful comment: "Yet within these calmly balanced lives dwelt also the pas-sion of religious exaltation and the tension of sexual frustration."

Although Shakers did not beget children of their own, they nurtured the children of others, always guid-ed by Mother Ann's law of love. In an era when a popu-lar parental motto was "love well, whip well," the Shakers exemplified Mother Ann's child-rearing doc-trine: "Little children are innocent, and they should never be brought out of it. If brought up in simplicity, they would receive good as easy as evil. Never speak to them in a passion; it will put devils into them."

People could not resist making fun of the Shakers' sexual abstinence. They said that Shakers must multiply by division, like amoebas, or expand by internal combustion, like steam engines. Artemus Ward, a popular humorist whose misspellings were considered hilarious in the nineteenth century, wrote, heavy-handedly:

> The Shakers is the strangest religious sex ever met. Why this jumpin up and singin and this antymatrimony idee?. . . My friends. . . you air neat and tidy. Your lands is flowin with milk and honey. Your brooms is fine, and your apple sass is honest. . . .You air honest in your dealins. You air quiet and don't distarb nobody. . . . Nothing ever conflicts with your pecooler idees — except when Human Nater busts out among you, as I understan she sumtimes do. . . . Here you air, all pend up by yerselves, talkin about the sins of a world you don't know nothin of.

Not surprisingly, the bold Shaker experiment in communal living attracted a stream of famous visitors. President James Monroe visited the Enfield family in New Hampshire. President Andrew Jackson went to South Union, Kentucky. Secretary of War Edwin Stanton went to New Lebanon, New York.

Some viewed them sympathetically, some did not. Ralph Waldo Emerson in his *Journals* depicts the Shakers "drudging in the fields and shuffling in their Bruin dance," but adds admiringly that these people were the pioneers of modern socialism who proved by example "not merely that successful communism is subjectively possible, but that this nation is free enough to let it grow."

Many writers were intrigued by the Believers. In *Moby Dick*, Herman Melville describes the archangel Gabriel as coming from "the crazy society of

Neskyeuna [*sic*] Shakers." Nathaniel Hawthorne's gloomy short story, "The Canterbury Pilgrim," denounces Shaker celibacy as unnatural. A young couple, seeking to become Believers, join a community "where all former ties have been sundered, all distinctions levelled." They are chilled to discover that Shakers have "substituted a cold and passionless security for mortal hope and fear, as in that other refuge of the world's weary outcasts, the grave."

No one was harder on the Shakers than Charles Dickens. In 1843, he visited the Mount Lebanon community in New York and said he felt about as much sympathy for the Believers "as if they had been so many figureheads of ships." His description of that community is Dickens at his most Dickensian:

> We walked into a grim room, where several grim hats were hanging on grim pegs, and the time was grimly told by a grim clock, which uttered every tick with a kind of struggle, as if it broke the grim silence reluctantly, and under protest. Ranged against the wall were six or eight stiff high-backed chairs, and they partook so strongly of the general grimness, that one would much rather have sat on the floor than incurred the smallest obligation to any of them.
>
> Presently, there strode into this apartment, a grim old Shaker, with eyes as hard and dull, and cold, as the great round metal buttons on his coat and waistcoat; a sort of calm goblin. . . . In the building where the Shaker manufactures were sold, the stock was presided over by something alive in a russet case, which the elder said was a woman; and

which I suppose *was* a woman, though I should not have suspected it.

Dickens concluded that if all Shaker women resembled the one he saw, any deviation from the rule of celibacy would be a "wild improbability."

On the other hand, there is praise from a wealthy member of the failed Brook Farm utopian experiment in Concord, Massachusetts. After visiting the Shakers, Charles Lane wrote Mrs. Bronson Alcott: "I think nowhere is the twofold purpose of human life, of being good and doing good, so fully provided for."

The Shakers' dedication to pacifism even attracted the interest of Count Leo Tolstoy in Russia. He wrote from Yasnaya Polyana to Elder Frederick Evans at Mount Lebanon: "I think the principle of nonresistance is the chief trait of true Christianity and the greatest difficulty in our times is to be true to it."

Shakerism was synonymous with peace, yet Mother Ann's early leadership in the peace movement has gone largely unrecognized. Along with the Quakers, she and her devout followers were the first Americans to stand for conscientious objection to warfare. They refused under any condition "to support the cause of war and bloodshed."

During the Civil War, some of the Believers were drafted into the Union army. Elder Evans and Elder Benjamin Gates made the long journey to Washington to petition President Lincoln, on the basis of the constitutional rights of conscience, for the exemption of the whole sect from fighting. Lincoln listened to the argument, then remarked that they should be made to fight, because the Union needed regiments of just such men.

But Abraham Lincoln understood the call of conscience. He granted the Shakers' Petition and the draftees were given an indefinite furlough. Doris Grumbach, in a *Commonweal* article called "American Peaceniks," makes an arresting statement: "The Shakers' most notable contribution to the life of this nation was, to my mind, their early impregnable pacifism and resolute conscientious objection."

It is easy to understand why women were attracted to Shakerism. The Believers' firm conviction that it takes *both* man and woman to complete the image of God was irresistible. Even angels and spirits were male and female. In the Shaker community there were no sexual stereotypes — women could be powerful and men could be tender.

It was a new way of living. Mother Ann may have been the first woman in America to possess real power. In a day of complete male dominance, she talked about the equality of women in a tough-minded way, calling for parity between male and female. It is not too far-fetched to say that Ann Lee, "the female Christ," was the founder of women's liberation in this country.

The Shaker movement was a protest against the ills of society. Emerson saw it as an important social experiment. He wrote in his *Journals* that the Shakers "were really the pioneers of modern socialism" whose example proved "not merely that successful communism is subjectively possible, but that this nation is free enough to let it grow." The Believers themselves, living by their adage *Give all you have and take only as you need,* thought they had started a new era of devout socialism, the age of the Millennial Church. But, as the historian Henri Desroche says, "It was only a dream which was later to be filed away in the company of other 'Utopias' that have fallen victim to the harsh facts of reality."

It is sad when a noble dream dies. For two hundred years, the Shakers *lived* Christianity instead of talking about it. Then twilight descended on the band of valiant idealists. Slowly the United Society of Believers in Christ's Second Appearing dwindled away. In 1909, there were a thousand members: by 1930, only a hundred; by 1950, a handful. Some Shaker sites are now museums, such as the one at Hancock, Massachusetts, which lovingly re-creates the Shaker way of life for visitors.

Mother Ann foresaw the eventual decline of the Millennial Church. She said, "There will come a time when there won't be enough Believers to bury their own dead. When only five are left, then there will be a revival." Sister Frances Carr of Sabbathday Lake says simply, "We'll go away in time, as will everybody. But our ideas and our way of life will never go away."

Today, the world's interest in the Shakers has progressed from curiosity about their mores, to concern about preserving their crafts, music, and architecture, to admiration and emulation of their "gift to be simple." Thomas Merton, the Catholic mystic, wrote: "After their departure these innocent people, who had once been so maligned, came to be regretted, loved and idealized. Too late, people . . . recognized the extraordinary importance of the spiritual phenomenon that had blossomed out in their midst. . . . The Shakers remain as witnesses to the fact that only humility keeps a man in communion with truth, and first of all with his own inner-truth. This one must know without knowing it, as they did."

And so Mother Ann's dream lives on . . .

Shaker Museums

Worldwide interest in the Shakers, and in their way of life, has led to the development of Shaker museums. The principal ones are listed below.

Kentucky
>Shakertown at Pleasant Hill, near Lexington
>Shakertown at South Union, near Bowling Green

Maine
>Sabbathday Lake, near Auburn

Massachusetts
>Fruitlands Museums, Harvard
>Hancock Shaker Village, near Pittsfield

New Hampshire
>Canterbury Shaker Village, Canterbury
>Lower Shaker Village, Enfield

New York
>Mount Lebanon Shaker Village, New Lebanon
>The Shaker Museum, Old Chatham
>Niskeyuna (Watervliet) Shaker Heritage Society,
>   near Albany

Ohio

The Golden Lamb, Lebanon
Kettering-Moraine Museum, Kettering
Shaker Historical Museum, Shaker Heights
Warren County Historical Society Museum,
   Lebanon

Noteworthy collections of Shaker artifacts are also on exhbit in the following places:

Kentucky Museum, Bowling Green, Kentucky
Metropolitan Museum of Art, New York,
   New York
Philadelphia Museum of Art, Philadelphia,
   Pennsylvania
Shelburne Museum, Burlington, Vermont
Western Reserve Historical Society, Cleveland,
   Ohio
Winterthur Museum, Winterthur, Delaware

Bibliography

Adams, Charles C. *The Community Industry of the Shakers*. Albany: State University of New York, 1932.

Allen, Arthur B. *Eighteenth Century England*. London: Rockliff, 1958.

Andrews, Edward D. and Faith. *Shaker Furniture: The Craftmanship of an American Communal Sect*. New Haven, Conn.: Yale University Press, 1937.

————. *Visions of the Heavenly Sphere: A Study in Shaker Religious Art*. Charlottesville : The University Press of Virginia, 1969.

Andrews, Edward D. *The Gift to Be Simple*. New York: J. J. Augustin, 1940.

————. *The People Called Shakers: A Search for the Perfect Society*. New York: Oxford University Press, 1953.

Axon, William E. A. "Biographical Notice of Ann Lee, A Manchester Prophetess and Founderess of the American Sect of the Shakers." *Transactions of the Historic Society of Lancashire and Cheshire*. Liverpool, England: 1875.

Bailey, Derrick S. *Sexual Relation in Christian Thought*. New York: Harper, 1959.

Bestor, Arthur. *Backwoods Utopias: The Sectarian Origins and the Owenite Phase of Communitarian Socialism in America : 1663–1829*. Philadelphia: University of Pennsylvania Press, 1953.

Blinn, Elder Henry Clay. *The Life and Gospel Experience of Mother Ann Lee*. East Canterbury, N.H.: Shakers, 1901.

Blumenthal, Walter Hart. *American Panorama: Pattern of the Past and Womanhood in Its Unfolding.* Worcester, Mass.: Achille J. St. Onge, 1962.

Brewer, Priscilla J. *Shaker Communities, Shaker Lives.* Hanover, N.H., and London: University Press of New England, 1986.

Brown, Thomas. *An Account of the People Called Shakers.* Troy, N.Y.: 1812.

Burr, Anna R. *Religious Confessions and Confessants.* Boston: Houghton Mifflin, 1914.

Commager, Henrv Steele. *The Search for a Usable Past.* New York: Knopf, 1967.

Cutten, George B. *The Psychological Phenomena of Christianity.* New York: Scribner's, 1908.

De Sanctis, Sante. *Religious Conversion.* New York: Harcourt, 1927.

Desroche, Henri. *The American Shakers.* Translated from French and edited by John K. Savacool. Amherst: University of Massachusetts Press, 1971.

Dexter, Elizabeth Anthony. *Colonial Women of Affairs: Women in Business and the Professions in America Before 1776.* Boston: Houghton Mifflin, 1931.

Dingwall, Eric J. *The American Woman: A Historical Study.* London: Duckworth, 1956.

Dyer, Mary Marshall. *A Portrait of Shakerism.* Concord, N.H.: 1822.

———. *The Rise and Progress of the Serpent from the Garden of Eden to the Present Day: With A DISCLOSURE OF SHAKERSIM.* Concord, N.H.: "Printed for the author," 1847.

Evans, Frederick William. *Autobiography of a Shaker.* Albany, N.Y.: 1869.

Faxon, Alicia Craig. *Women and Jesus.* Philadelphia: United Church Press, 1973.

Flexner, Eleanor. *Century of Struggle: The Woman's Rights Movement in the United States.* Cambridge: Harvard University Press, 1966.

Fowles, John. *A Maggot.* Boston: Little, Brown, 1985.

Green, Calvin, and Wells, Seth Y. *A Summary View of the Millennial Church of the United Society of Believers (Commonly called Shakers).* Albany, N.Y.: Packard & van Benthuysen, 1823.

Harkness, Georgia. *Women in Church and Society.* Nashville, Tenn.: Abington Press, 1972.

Hutton, Daniel M. *Old Shakertown and the Shakers.* Harrodsburg, Ky.: Harrodsburg Herald Press, 1936.

James, William. *The Varieties of Religious Experience.* London: Longmans, Green, 1902.

Johnson, Paul E. *Psychology of Religion.* Nashville, Tenn: Abington Press, 1960.

Ketchum, Richard M., ed. *The American Heritage History of the American Revolution.* New York: American Heritage, 1971.

Lamson, David R. *Two Years' Experience among the Shakers.* West Boylston: AMS Press, 1848. (Published by the author.)

Langdon-Davies, John. *A Short History of Women.* New York: Viking, 1927.

Lassiter, William Lawrence. *Shaker Architecture.* New York: Bonanza Books, 1966.

Mace, Aurelia G. *The Aletheia: Spirit of Truth.* Farmington, Me.: Knowlton and McLeary, 1907.

Melcher, Marguerite Fellows. *The Shaker Adventure.* Princeton, N.J.: Princeton University Press, 1941.

Morse, Flo. *The Shakers and the World's People.* Hanover, N.H., and London: University Press of New England, 1987.

Neal, Julia. *By Their Fruits*. Chapel Hill: University of North Carolina Press, 1947.

Newman, Cathy. "The Shakers Brief Eternity." *National Geographic Magazine*, Sept. 1989.

Nordhoff, Charles. *The Communistic Societies of the United States*. New York: Harper, 1875.

Oxley, William. *Modern Messiahs and Wonder Workers*. London: Trubner, 1889.

Reeder, Colonel Red. *The Story of the American Revolution*. New York: Duell, Sloan and Pearce, 1959.

Rourke, Constance. *The Roots of American Culture*. New York: Harcourt, 1942.

Rudin, Josef. *Fanaticism: A Psychological Analysis*. Notre Dame, Ind.: Notre Dame Press, 1969.

Sanders, John. *Manchester*. London: Hart-Davis, 1967.

Spaulding, E. Wilder. *New York in the Critical Period 1783–1789*. New York: Columbia University Press, 1932.

Svmonds, John. *Thomas Brown and the Angels*. London: Hutchinson, 1961.

Testimonies Concerning the Character and Ministry of Mother Ann Lee and the First Witnesses of the Gospel of Christ's Second Appearing; Given by Some of the Aged Brethern and Sisters of the United Society. Edited by S. Y. Wells. Albany, N.Y.: Packard & van Benthuysen, 1827.

Testimonies of the Life, Character, Revelations and Doctrines of Our Ever Blessed Mother Ann Lee, and the Elders with Her; Through Whom the Word of Eternal Life was Opened in This Day of Christ's Second Appearing: Collected From Living Witnesses, by Order of the Ministry, in Union with the Church. Hancock, Mass.: J. Tallcott & J. Deming, Junre, 1816.

White, Anna, and Taylor, Lelia. *Shakerism: Its Meaning and Message*. Columbus, Ohio: 1905.

Youngs, Benjamin Seth. *The Testimony of Christ's Second Appearing; Containing a General Statement of All Things Pertaining to the Faith and Practice of the Church of God in This Latter-day.* . . . Lebanon, Ohio: 1808.

Index

Nardi Reeder Campion has written for such publications as the *New York Times Magazine, New Yorker, American Heritage, Family Circle, Gourmet, Boston Globe Magazine, Life, Sports Illustrated, Yankee,* and *Harvard Magazine.* She is co-author with her brother, Colonel Red Reeder, of *Bringing Up the Brass* (1951), filmed as *The Long Gray Line,* and *West Point Story* (1956), and with Rosamond W. Stanton of *Look to This Day! The Lively Education of a Great Woman Doctor, Connie Guion, M.D.* (1965). She is author of *Kit Carson, Pathfinder of the West* (1963), and *Casa Means Home* (1970). Her *Patrick Henry: Firebrand of the Revolution* (1961) has been translated into eight languages. She has also written biographies for *Encyclopaedia Britannica* and *World Book.* This is a new edition of her book published in 1976 as *Ann the Word.*